SCIENCE, ORIGINS, & ANCIENT CIVILIZATIONS

Scientific Evidence Withheld
from School Textbooks

Gerry Burney

Target Truth Ministries.com

Update 2014
Update 2019

Science, Origins, & Ancient Civilizations
Scientific Evidence Withheld from School Textbooks
by Gerry Burney

Printed in the United States of America.

ISBN 13: 978-1-60791-625-3

Unless otherwise indicated, Bible quotations are taken from the King James Version (KJV). Copyright © 1999 by Zondervan.

Gerry Burney
Target Truth Ministries.com
Box 1299
burneyfam@prodigy.net
Ukiah, Calif.
95482

Gerry Burney graduated from San Francisco State University with a degree in Interdisciplinary Studies, and pursued graduate study at the University of California at Berkeley and seminary study with the Southern Baptist Seminary in Tennessee. He authored his first book on economics and poverty in 1985. Mr. Burney is a veteran of the U.S. Air Force, and served in Thailand in 1968, and Vietnam in 1969. He retired from managing microwave communication technologies for over thirty years. He has pastored in several Baptist churches within the Mendo-Lake association of churches in California, and is currently the chaplain to the inmates for the Mendocino County Jail and Juvenile Hall. He has been a high school teacher and teaches seminars on biblical studies. He also operates an outreach to prisons with weekly studies, sent at no cost to prisoners.

www.xulonpress.com

TABLE OF CONTENTS

INTRODUCTION

"Let no one in any way deceive you, for it (the end times), will not come unless the *apostasy* comes first..."

2 Thess. 2:1-3; Matt. 24:12

What might be the signs of the apostasy?

A) <u>Jesus, as fully God</u>, is either not a priority discussed in church, or is even denied by some churches.

B) <u>The Atonement of Christ</u> as the *primary* message of the church, is replaced with a message primarily of good deeds and meeting human needs (poverty, environment, health care, tolerance, etc.—"social justice").

C) <u>Separation of church and state</u>, as interpreted today (which was *not* the understanding of the Founding Fathers), seeks to *exclude* God from all government programs and even education.

D) <u>Sex outside the marriage of one man and one woman</u>, is *accepted* by most people, even some Christians. Marriage and divorce were *never* designed by God as a right, but rather, to represent our fallen nature and need for God. People cannot be given equal status in life by governments. Marriage and divorce *primarily* represent God's plan of salvation and judgment.

E) <u>Abortion</u> is accepted by society as a right by most people (Here, man becomes a god, determining when life begins). Over 60 million babies have been killed since abortion was legalized in America. Ironically, this is double the number of illegal aliens the country seems to need, in order to care for the generation which has aborted the babies.

F) <u>Euthanasia</u> (legal suicide), is accepted by many. Man, here, becomes a god, determining when life ends.

G) *Macro*-evolution is worshiped in place of God. Man is elevated to the "highest form of life" by believing in macro-evolution. Macro-evolution is actually a religion, as it requires faith (there is *no* scientific proof, only a hypothesis). Additionally, scientific evidence which actually *denies* macro-evolution has been *deleted* from education. Christianity, on the other hand, is *not* a religion—it is a relationship, and welcomes all evidence.

God's Word tells us that we are sinners at *conception*, and all have been condemned by God to hell, even before we are born. This is not because of our ancestor's sin (Adam), as taught by many today, but because we each are individually, personally, responsible for our sin (**original sin**), in Eden (141). God loves His creation, therefore, God **predestined** a plan to reconcile with those who have fallen, if they will change and trust in Jesus. God *re*-created this earth (the 7-day event—141), to provide for this period of reconciliation. This period of reconciliation includes Satan, who has also fallen. Satan imitates God in order to deceive many into rejecting Jesus, and accepting false religions. Satan persuades many to have faith in science, which is based upon limited knowledge, or to accept human desires such as sex, wealth, health, fame, status, etc., as *priorities* in life, in order to detour our true need to trust in Christ, in order to avoid hell. There is a specific number of beings to be born into this flesh existence, and then God will usher in the end judgment. God will destroy this creation, and bring about a return to Eden (the new heaven and earth--141).

<u>The apostasy is here</u>, and that number to be born will soon be reached. Israel is God's timepiece, and the clock was reset in 1948.

The end-times are upon us, and this, more than likely, is the generation to see Christ return, and the judgment take place. Don't be deceived by philosophies, with no evidence to support their claims or understandings of life and death. A dialogue is good, but without the *truth*, dialoguing is worthless. Truth is exclusive. There can be only one truth. Those who point to "other truths" are uninformed (one of Satan's tactics). Please share these books, studies, and messages at <u>Target Truth Ministries.com</u> with others to help inform the multitudes who are lost, spiritually weak, and heading to hell.

God has predestined a millennium to provide a way for those who (during this lifetime), haven't heard the call to Christ, in order to receive their opportunity for salvation (142, 144). Only those who trust in Christ will avoid hell. Many in this life have been deceived by Satan's imitation faiths (143).

If theology is not clear to you (which even many theologians haven't figured God's plan out yet), and if you are concerned about the fate of humankind, your family, and neighbors, please share these books, studies, and messages of God's plan with them. These books and studies are for those who are searching God's Word for the truth, and truly concerned with humankind's eternal state, whether it be heaven or hell. All will live eternally, either in the presence of their Creator, or separated to spend all eternity isolated, alone, forever in outer darkness. Satan even has people thinking that hell will either be a place where all beings there will be grouped together to be able to make the best of the situation, or that hell doesn't really exist. However, God is clear. Hell is eternal darkness, being alone, and separated from God and loved ones who trust in Jesus. Eternal isolation is the justice determined for those who have sinned against their Creator, who is eternal. We are *all* sinners, and *all* condemned, but God offers us reconciliation, and life with Him in His kingdom, if we will *trust* in Him.

Pastor Gerry Burney
Box 1299
Ukiah, Calif. 95482

Target Truth Ministries.com
<u>burneyfam@prodigy.net</u>

Please make tax deductible <u>donations</u> payable to: Crossroads Church, and mail to above P.O. Box or Target Truth Ministries. com (or Pay-Pal), to help us spread the truth.

This ministry is dedicated to God's Word and providing scripturally-based answers to theological questions which have puzzled scholars for hundreds of years. The result is a unique understanding using the whole of Scripture to reveal the truth.

Daniel 12:4

<u>Science & Origins</u>

<u>Creation & Evolution</u>

<u>Civilizations & Ancient Man</u>

See *Target Truth Ministries.com* for News & Updates

PARADIGMS &
CONVENTIONAL WISDOM

See *Target Truth Ministries.com*
for News & Updates

O nce, a few hundred years ago, people trusted in the clergy. The clergy insisted that the sun revolved around the earth. Galileo (a believer in Jesus), provided proof that this was not true. Note that the Bible does not say the sun revolves around the earth—this was just a tradition of the authorities at that time. Galileo took issue with the leadership—he did not have an issue with Jesus or the Bible. But, the result was that people began losing trust in the Bible (the supernatural), and began to trust science instead (the natural).

Fast-forward to today—people are trusting in science more than ever. From the beginning, many Christians (including Galileo and many other scientists), searched for the truth, while others held to tradition. Ironically, science today has assumed the role of the clergy of old—trusting in traditions and theories of man, over scientific proofs and evidence. Science is *speculating* about the origins of the universe and the origins of life, just as the clergy of old speculated about the earth and sun. Science has actually chosen to ignore evidence which contradicts the conventional evolutionary hypothesis of origins of both the universe and life (just as the old church ignored evidence—holding to tradition). Therefore, people today, are once again trusting in man's beliefs, and not the truth.

Any physics textbook, when referring to the origin of the universe, will state as Einstein did, that during that first short period of time after the "Big Bang," the laws of physics were suspended (translation—it was supernatural—not natural). So also, with life. Even the Noble scientist in DNA research, Dr. Francis Crick, has stated that there is no "natural" way for DNA to have arisen— DNA is a four-bit binary code, and needs to be organized and programmed. His only explanation for life is that it must have come from outer space (again, leaning toward some "natural" origin even though it remains "unknown").

Today, people are not trusting in a solid foundation of rock (actual scientific proof), but upon the sand of opinion (hypothesis, speculation, and tradition). The Bible does give us actual proof of its supernatural origins. Great prophecies such as that of Daniel 9, Ezekiel 4, and others (verified by science and history with the discovery of the Dead Sea Scrolls, which date to hundreds of years prior to Jesus, and over 2,000 years prior to the restoral of Israel in 1948), give us conclusive proof of prophecies being fulfilled exactly—in many cases to the very day—over hundreds of years. The exact fulfillment of these prophecies proves the authenticity of God's Word, whereas, science can only offer hypothesis and even ignores much of the scientific evidence.

Christians are in the place that Galileo was in, centuries ago. The authority in control (clergy then, and science today), are suppressing the truth. Fortunately, (for Galileo and for us), the Bible has always offered the truth for those interested. Galileo trusted it, and I trust it.

To quote Albert Einstein, "Science without religion is lame, and religion without science is blind." We need both to see clearly.

As we go through various interpretations of science and the Bible, one will note that one of the all-time greatest scientific and historical landmarks of humankind is totally absent from God's Word. Furthermore, this absence must be deliberate on God's part, because if writing the Bible were left to humans alone, we couldn't help but focus on this landmark.

This landmark forms the foundation for much of science and history, including astronomy, mathematics, anthropology, etc. This landmark is one of the seven wonders of the world. This landmark dates back to when humans were just emerging from the Stone Age. And, yet, the Bible, which also traces its history back thousands and thousands of years, and makes hundreds of references to Egypt, both in the Old and New Testaments, never once mentions the Great Pyramids or the Sphinx.

Why?

Some scholars refer to the biblical passage in Isaiah 19:18-22 as an indication the pyramids were built by the early generations of Adam and Seth. However, this text fails as a biblical reference to the pyramids because it does not specify the altar as a pyramid structure and, more importantly, the context of the passages are in reference to the future end-times.

Why should such a dominant part of human history and culture be totally left out of the Bible, when much of the Bible's setting is in Egypt itself?

This anomaly will become crystal clear as one explores all the books in this series: *Eden to Evil, Revelation, Apostasy, End-Times, & "This Generation," God's Plan / Satan's Plan,* and *The Book of ..Chronologies & Time Charts* (Target Truth Ministries.com).

In the last one hundred years or so, the governmental educational establishment has made a conscious decision to approve of "conventional" science, and to dismiss the Bible and the evidence supporting it. Education today is government dominated and must restrict any reference to God.

Those who dismiss the Bible accept the view or paradigm of conventional science. Scientists fall into one of two "paradigms," meaning one of two various views of measuring time and age. One view, or paradigm, uses *evidence* to show a young age for the world. I will call this view **Paradigm B**. Another view, or paradigm (which is the dominant conventional view today), tries to weave only "acceptable" evidence into a *theory* of long time periods of evolution of the universe and life, while ignoring the evidence against long time periods. This I will call **Paradigm A** — the dominate public education position.

Very few people dig deep, research, and seek out answers from *both* the original biblical texts in Hebrew or Greek, and the *total* of scientific evidences from various disciplines.

The purpose of this series of books is to develop a deeper understanding of God's Word, rather than just dismissing it, as is the trend today. To do this, one must look at science as well as the Bible, and, where the Bible is concerned, one must focus on both Genesis and Revelation, to see the relevance science has to the Bible.

The bottom line is that Jesus was resurrected from death, and then, over the next several weeks, Jesus appeared to *hundreds* of people, to prove He had overcome death and now lives (Acts 1:1-8, 1 Cor. 15:1-8). Evidence of this abounds (84, 90). People born after 1970 have no problem believing a man walked on the moon, even though there was only one eyewitness. There were hundreds who witnessed Christ alive after he had been executed. Furthermore,

Jesus made frequent references to the Old Testament, and these references by Christ, who was able to overcome death, support the authority of the Old Testament.

Christ also showed us how things are created mature, created with age, therefore, showing us how our universe and life could also be created with evidence of age from the very beginning (John 2:3-11; Matt. 14:17-20).

Science is at a loss to explain God, and therefore, must theorize that the universe and life began from some mythical "spark," even though science cannot explain where the "original material" codes came from that formed complex DNA, or the universe, for that matter.

One can deny the Bible all one wants, but evidence being gathered by scientists actually supports what the Bible says.

The Bible is completely understandable, without any scientific knowledge. Time and time again, the Bible makes reference to things like weather patterns, ocean currents, and wind currents, which weren't scientifically proven until the time of Benjamin Franklin. The Bible referred to these, thousands of years ago (Eccl. 1:6; Job 36:27-28; Ps. 8:8). Until 1993, and the C.O.B.E. satellite mission, science couldn't provide evidence of the universe being stretched, but the Bible told of this phenomenon thousands of years ago (Isa. 40:22, 42:5, 45:12, 51:13; Jer. 10:12). In 2 Peter 3:10, we read of elements melting away, and back then, people could not believe that the elements could ever be destroyed.

The Bible also made reference to the earth being a sphere (not flat), long before science could prove it, or anyone even believed it (Isa. 40:22).

Science knows that some unknown force (called "dark matter" or "dark energy") holds all atoms and the entire universe together. The Bible gives the source for that force in Colossians 1:13-17—God.

Studies in 1996 (which continue to be updated and verified), and cited by David M Rohl, in a book titled: *"Pharaohs and Kings,"* indicate that the conventional Egyptian dating method may be off by 300 years (more or less), around the period of the twenty-first dynasty. This is giving new support to the authenticity of the Bible, all the way back to Genesis. It would appear that Egyptology had the science of chronology wrong all these years and the "new" chronology actually proves the Bible was correct all the time.

Conversely......

Science is not understandable without the Bible. Theories of age, evolution, geology, and catastrophic occurrences are not properly understood without the Bible as the reference point. Even today, there is no scientific theory for where the matter for the supposed "Big Bang" came from. It's just somehow there. One will note that all scientific studies of age still are referred to as *theories*, and are not proven. Some theories are "preferred" over others, and these preferred theories receive funding for study.

One notable scientist shared a theory with other scientists, which closely follows the Bible's description of destruction in Revelation. His name was Albert Einstein, and the theory is crustal displacement. This same theory is used to explain the existence of fossil forests frozen under (over a mile of ice in Antarctica), an ice layer which is still growing today, even though the northern ice cap is shrinking.

Albert Einstein's premise is somewhat unconventional in the scientific community, as were many of his theories, and therefore, it hasn't attracted much money for studies. Grant funding tends to go towards the more conventional areas of the Big Bang, black holes, and life on other planets, which are popular today. Theories such as Earth-Crust Displacement (detailed in the geology section), which Albert Einstein and others supported, are still *not* part of the "conventional" scientific approach. These "unconventional" theories fit with the biblical understanding of earth, life and age, but the "conventional" scientific community has not approved of any paradigm outside their own.

The "conventional" scientific paradigm, however, is slowly changing today. This is primarily due to recent discoveries of meteor and asteroid activity having occurred, not only in the distant past, when the universe was supposedly more active, but activity which has occurred *recently* in the earth's history. This recent activity suggests to scientists today that the earth's history is *not* just uniform (which was the conventional theory for decades), but that catastrophic events can occur even today, which can dramatically change the earth and life overnight. After 2005, a small group of researchers at Stanford University began to re-examine this theory of Earth-Crust Displacement.

Theories of evolution of life are changing also, due to evidence that shows that all life forms appeared suddenly in the geologic fossil record. In December 1995, in an article entitled: *"Evolution's Big Bang,"* in *Time* magazine, the problem science faces is clearly stated: *"Understanding what made the Cambrian explosion possible doesn't address the larger question of what made it happen so fast. Here, scientists delicately slide across data-thin ice, suggesting scenarios that are based on intuition rather than solid evidence."* In 2007, evolutionists reporting on *Trilobites*, recognized that most variability amongst the animals was actually in the past, at the beginning, during the Cambrian "explosion." Evolution predicts that we should see more varieties as the millions of years progressed, and as the species developed, but actual evidence in the fossil record doesn't support this. There are many times fewer varieties in existence today, than during the beginning, in the Cambrian. Life is actually devolving, not evolving.

So, the purpose in this series of books, is not to dismiss the evidence, but to try and relate the evidence to what the Bible describes in Genesis and Revelation. Of course, our understanding of Genesis and Revelation is also subject to "conventional" pressures to interpret them in an "approved" way.

One presumption is that the Bible says everything was created in seven days, and that places the age of the earth at 6,000-13,000 years. When one studies the original Hebrew, one soon discovers how we have oversimplified Genesis. Many of us have been raised under a paradigm of this seven-day creation. The seven-day creation is correct. *But*, is it the whole story? (141)

Another presumption is that science has proof of billions of years for the age of the universe and evolution. In fact, there are two schools of scientific thought on this question of age, whether old or young. Each of these scientific theories has many evidences to support them.

One school of thought *requires* billions of years, while the other school requires only thousands. The word "requires" is used because there seems to be no in-between. This is because these two paradigms are based on a belief either in billions of years (with mostly uniform slow growth and evolution of life), or, conversely, the biblical seven days. We either have long time periods for life's evolution, or 6,000-13,000 years of generations found in the Bible. Two different, yet, "conventional" views.

Take your choice.

It is interesting that scientists tend to form on one side of the argument or the other. No in-between.

Most scientists, who accept the theory of billions of years for formation of the universe, also tend to accept the theory of evolution and slow change, requiring billions of years.

Other scientists point to evidence that shows that *macro*-evolution (a *new* kind of life – a *new* set of DNA codes forming from the old life form), could have *never* taken place, that the fossil record shows *no* evidence of *macro*-evolution. These scientists tend to look to evidence showing a very young earth and universe in the range of 6,000-15,000 years.

Of course, the generally accepted conventional theory is billions of years, even though science cannot prove it.

7

Today, science is arguing with science. This is clearly shown by the "dawn of civilization" conflict. One group of scientists argues that evidence shows that there must have been a high level of knowledge required to build the pyramids, the Sphinx, create the Aztec math and astronomical calendar, and many other unexplainable phenomena, while conventional science argues that early humans, barely out of the stone age, built them all.

When the world was supposedly just emerging from the Stone Age, it's interesting to note that the Great Pyramid of Egypt had each of its sides constructed with a curvature inward, to signify the exact curvature of the earth. This is significant because, at this early date, most supposedly thought that the earth was flat.

The biblical community is put in a quandary. If one accepts "conventional" science, then one must dump the Bible. And, the media and educational establishment make almost no mention of other evidence, other paradigms—actual evidence pointing to a young earth.

Genesis (origins) is not the only book of the Bible that has a conventional view and a minority view.

Just as one can be deceived by science, concerning Genesis (origins), one can also be deceived by science about Revelation (end-times). Science would have us ignore God's prophecy (in Revelation), of Christ's return, a final judgment, this world's destruction and a new heaven and earth. Science sees the world as part of an evolving process up to this point, and it is now beginning to head to destruction, all according to natural processes, with no intervention by a God necessary. Conventional science sees the world ending gradually as the sun grows old, or by the universe either collapsing or expanding forever, or even, perhaps, human beings destroying everything themselves. Science denies any involvement by God in either the creation, or the end of the universe.

But recent scientific evidence is beginning to recognize that the earth and solar system can change suddenly. Scientifically, an end to life on earth, as we know it, could occur at any moment.

The truly sad result of these conventional paradigms is that they drown out any deeper understanding of the biblical message and other scientific evidences.

The point of having a clear understanding of creation and the end-times is to *avoid being deceived* into thinking science has all the answers, when science itself is in debate. Too many are abandoning God's Word, under a false assumption that science has proven the Bible wrong.

Is there any possibility of science and the Bible actually agreeing?

We will discover in these pages that there is plenty of evidence to support only thousands of years for the age of life. The billions of years theory is not proven. The same is true of fossil evidence. There is *no* fossil evidence of *macro*-evolution. Life could, in fact, only be thousands of years old. So, these issues are really wide open. Of course, one would hardly know the issues are wide open, if one listens only to our governmental educational and media sources. The scientific community, however, struggles with age, evolution, and the dawn of civilization arguments continually.

Conventional science, while holding firm to long time periods for the universe, is in disagreement over evolution and life. As the knowledge science accumulates keeps unfolding, it seems that *macro*-evolution (evolution from one life form to another), never occurred. Especially, as no fossil evidence has ever been found. There is no proof at all. The fossil record shows similarities between different kinds, but no transition from one kind to another. To this date, all proposed transitions have proven to be invalid to most scientists. Even DNA analysis does not support *Macro*-evolution.

When science does speak of "proof" of evolution, it is *micro*-evolution, of the type where birds may produce a different size beak from one generation to the next, as they breed together. This is not the creation of a new kind evolving from other kinds. This *micro*- evolution is not in conflict with the Bible and life following its kind. A bird with a larger beak can still breed with a bird of the same kind that has a smaller beak, just as humans of any race can marry together; we humans are all one kind.

The same problem of conventional thought also exists in the study of the Bible. Paradigms prevail, including the seven-day creation and the pre-tribulation rapture.

The Bible itself provides us with the indications that, while the creation of Genesis1:3-2:3 is most likely a literal period of seven twenty-four hour days, there are also references to other periods of creation, with no mention of time limits (91, 92, 93, 95, 96, 141, 143). Also, as mentioned earlier, the word "rapture," in reference to the end times, could apply to an event, either before or after all the tribulation and destruction (142, 144).

Today, there is only a minority who allow that perhaps the universe came into existence at some relatively distant point in time,

and that life, as we know it, came into existence only within the last 15,000 years, or even less.

And, few could have conceived that destruction, of the type written of in Revelation, could ever occur scientifically, although, there is currently a new look being taken at catastrophic events in the earth's recent geologic history.

So, what will it be?

The conventional view of the Bible, a book written thousands of years ago and largely skimmed over today? (A book, by the way, not easily understood and often *doubted* by many).

Or......

The conventional view of the earth, with science promoting the theories of the Big Bang, some kind of life "spark," evolution from fish to humans, and eventually, earth's destruction? (Not provable theories, but nevertheless, *accepted by many*).

Or......

Are science and the Bible reconcilable?

I think one will find we've failed in both areas of science and the Bible, trying too hard to prove a point over evolution one way or the other.

The conventional understanding of Genesis and Revelation is too simplistic and tends to try to ignore science, when science actually supports the Bible. If one ignores the Bible, because biblical scholars ignore science, there is a real possibility one will be deceived into worshiping science. And, if being deceived is a concern, then one needs to have a fuller understanding of God's message and how it relates to science.

The conventional understanding of science and assumptions of evolution, long ages, and the denial of super intelligence existing during the past Stone Age period, don't really match up with the evidence, either from a *physical sciences* perspective or from an *evidences of civilization* perspective. Bible scholars and scientists may be too busy defending their paradigms, and ignoring each other's contributions, to truly understand God's whole picture.

But.....

Throughout this series of books, we will examine the relationship of science to the Bible's view of age, history, and our future, in the context of God's plan of redemption and reconciliation.

I think one will find we've failed in both areas of science and the Bible, trying too hard to prove a point over evolution one way or the other.

Why is there no reference in the Bible to the pyramids and the Sphinx, when Egypt is referred to hundreds of times, both in the Old and New Testaments?

AGE/SCIENCE PARADIGM

See the **Globe Time Chart** in the Appendix.
See *Target Truth Ministries.com*
for <u>News & Updates</u>

There is a myth that science is the study of natural processes, and therefore, because creation is considered supernatural, it cannot be considered science to study it. However, science is the gathering of *knowledge*, and not limited to natural processes alone. Science should be the search for *truth*—the study of all resources.

<u>Definition</u>:

We will address here the issue of *"age"* and the two basic opposing scientific views. Note the usage of the terms "paradigm A" and "paradigm B," to describe two distinctive scientific approaches.

Paradigm A: is <u>the conventional scientific view of *age* today</u>. This view is the popular one. The media and educational texts usually refer to these theories. These theories receive the bulk of all research money. These theories represent a linear view of development of the cosmos, evolution, and life, going from under-developed to developed, from disorder to order, from simple to complex. On the subject of "age," paradigm A is based on *theory* more than evidence.

Paradigm B: is the other view of *age*. This scientific approach uses evidence that is verifiable and makes no assumption that the cosmos or life is evolving in a linear form. In fact, paradigm B researchers find the evidence seems to indicate a slow process of *deterioration*, just as the laws of thermodynamics have proven—everything going from order to disorder, from complex to simple. Paradigm B is based on evidence.

This age/science study is broken down into the various areas that are related to the understanding of *time* (age), as it relates to the origins of the universe, as well as the origins of mankind.

AGE OF THE UNIVERSE AND SOLAR SYSTEM

See *Target Truth Ministries.com*
for <u>News & Updates</u>

S cientific studies of the Big Bang refer to the first few seconds or minutes as a period when the laws of physics were suspended. This is another way of saying "supernatural," except a scientist (if they want to keep their job), cannot use the word "supernatural." This word is too close to "God." Therefore, when you read a scientific study, it will refer to the laws of physics being "suspended."

It seems every time scientists think they have a theory to explain an old age for origins of the universe and evolution, that new questions and problems arise.

As a result of the Hubble Space Telescope project, in February and March of 1995, all scientific reports were focused on not one, but two crises. These studies show: 1) A paradox where the universe seems to be younger than the stars that are in it and, 2) A huge chunk of the universe is headed in the wrong direction—not expanding ever-outward, but heading directly toward some distant point, beyond the constellation Orion at 1.56 million miles per hour. Andromeda, our closest galaxy, is approaching us at 300,000 miles per hour. Both Andromeda and our galaxy are heading toward the Virgo super cluster. Current Big Bang theory requires a smooth expansion of the entire universe, but science doesn't find this.

There is almost no disagreement between conventional scientists on methods, and results, of measuring the age of stars. However, these same scientists disagree over the density of the universe. A high density means a younger universe, and it seems more and more density is continually showing up as a result of studies beginning in 2003.

Teams of scientists from Wendy Freedman's team of the Carnegie Observatories in Pasadena, to Mark Lacy's team at Oxford University in Britain, to Byron Spinrad of the University of California, George Jacoby and Richard Griffith, of the Space Telescope Science Institute in Baltimore, Maryland, all confess that science now has no adequate theory to explain how the universe began, much less when. New observations and evidence are destroying the current Big Bang theories, and there is nothing conventional science can offer in its place.

Just a year prior to the Hubble discoveries, evidence gathered by the COBE Satellite, *CO*smic *B*ackground *E*xplorer, and analyzed by Edward Wright of UCLA, Charles Bennett of Goddard Space Flight Center, Astrophysicist Joel Primack of U.C. Santa Cruz, and George Smoot, Astrophysicist with the California Lawrence Berkeley Lab (1), supports the theory that the universe came into being and did the bulk of its expansion, as we know it today, in *one-thousandth of one second*. COBE collects microwaves, which, it is theorized, were formed from light waves that were stretched out when the universe was formed in that first fraction of one second.

Yuri Izotov, in 1999, in the *Astrophysical Journal* wrote of the helium abundance in certain galaxies, and noted that by the time the universe was one millisecond old, it was cooled down into a sea of protons and neutrons, and within twenty seconds, one fourth of the hydrogen, by mass, would have converted into helium and other elements.

Dr. Gerald Schroeder, Nuclear Physicist, has established the exponential expansion factor of the universe at 10^{12}, and this means the universe was established in a matter of days. Alan Guths, in "*The Inflationary Universe*," gives the figure of 10^{20} which is even faster. Astronomer Joseph Silk in "*The Big Bang*" agrees with

Schroeder that 10^{12} is the factor. It is interesting that 10^{12} is equal to six days of time as measured by earth gravity, when compared to gravity in space during the Big Bang.

One of the proofs of the Big Bang model is theorized to be the CMB—Cosmic Microwave Background radiation, which was discovered in 1964, and won the Noble Prize for Penzias and

Wilson. The theory is that the microwave radiation is the afterglow of the Big Bang, and what we measure today passes through galaxies, thus distorting it—in other words, the CMB we are seeing is a "shadow" of the Big Bang. However, in 2015, a group of scientists led by Dr. Richard Lieu pointed out in a study of 31 galaxy clusters that the "shadow" effect was missing. The study found that the CMB must be local, and not from any theorized Big Bang. Their conclusion is that something else is going on—the data do not support the theory of the Big Bang.

The current theory is, our universe we see today originated out of nothing tangible. Matter existed in the form of energy. Einstein theorized, and science has since shown, that energy becomes matter as it expands and slows. As energy consolidates, it reaches a critical mass. The forces are pulling so strong, that it is like a black hole, where even light energy cannot escape. When critical mass occurs, then energy explodes and a hyper-inflation (or stretching), takes place. Energy blows right through the event horizon (and, in effect, becomes a white hole, from where light escapes). The event horizon is that point where the pull of gravity is not so strong as to pull the light back. As matter escapes, the event horizon shrinks inward. The energy from this event includes extremely high frequency energy—much higher than the frequency spectrum of light. The universe does the bulk of its expansion in the very first second of this expansion or stretching event.

We should note that the term "stretching of the heavens" appears seventeen times in Scripture (Isa. 40:21-22). According to science, in this process of stretching, space expands faster than the speed of light, while at the same time, matter within the inflation can only reach a limited percentage of the speed of light—estimated by conventional science to be a maximum of 80 percent.

In another similar theory, Humphreys, in the book *"Starlight & Time,"* suggests that earth is actually at the center of the mass of the cosmos. The greater the velocity of expansion, the slower is time, and in the beginning, with earth being at the center of the mass of the cosmos, the outer masses would inflate in distance, exponentially up to **10^{20}** times the speed of light. He calls this "Gravitational Time Dilation." This effect of time dilation has been tested scientifically with experiments conducted by J. C. Hafele, and Richard Keating using cesium clocks, which proved Einstein's theory. This would account for the billions of years of "distance" being accomplished in only hours.

Let's try some math:

$$10^1 = 10$$
$$10^2 = 100$$
$$10^{12} = 1,000,000,000,000$$

If age (using current observations of speed of light) appears to be 14,000,000,000 years (per conventional science), and we round up a year to 400 days (for math simplicity), and multiply the days times the years—we get 5,600,000,000,000 total days (in 14 billion years). Per science, the stretch/inflation factor is around 10^{12}, which means the actual time for the beginning of the universe would be about 5.6 days! If the stretch factor was as great as 10^{20} as suggested by some, then the time needed for creation would be even less.

Measurements in 2018 establish that the inflation rate today between galaxies is slower, relative to each other, than in the past. Today, there is only a three percent difference between our time, and the time of the outer masses, some of which were up to eighty percent of the speed of light early after the "big bang" event.

Reports in 2019, as a result of work by Dr. John Hartnett upon earlier work by cosmologist Dr. Moshe Carmeli, suggest Time Dilation doesn't even need gravitational effects to account for seemingly long periods of the age of the cosmos (14 billion years as compared to days). Time dilation could simply be related to the enormous accelerated stretching of the fabric of space. In other words, clocks located in the outer reaches of the expanding universe would run exceedingly fast (giving the appearance of billions of years), as compared to a clock here on earth. Under this analysis, light from distant galaxies could reach earth in a matter of days of earth time (Genesis 1:14-19).

The evidence from COBE does not conflict with scientists using either paradigm A or B, as defined in the introduction. Scientists using paradigm A (conventional science), theorize that after that first instant of time, when the great expansion took place, it then took billions of years for gravity to form clumps of matter and gases into galaxies. Scientists using paradigm B (young age for creation), find no evidence of billions of years being necessary after that first second of time. Many theories of age of the universe are being offered, some requiring billions of years, and some showing evidence of only thousands of years. They are all theories.

Current Big Bang models attempt to use "dark matter" and "dark energy" to explain what we see happening in the universe. First, science measured the density of all matter visible in the universe, and they realized that there was not enough "known" matter to hold the universe together. The gravitational influence of stars and planets is measurable, and it is not sufficient to keep the universe from flying apart. Per science, about ninety-five percent of the matter needed to hold things together is *missing*. So, science called this missing matter "dark matter." In the late 1990's, science discovered that the expansion of the universe is actually speeding up, not stabilized, or slowing down as had be theorized. In other words, there had to be something that was offsetting the "dark matter," which was supposed to pull things together, and stabilize them. So, science called this force speeding up the expansion "dark energy." Today, science theorizes that visible matter accounts for five percent of all matter, "dark matter" accounts for twenty-five percent of matter needed, and "dark energy" accounts for seventy percent of the missing force (Col. 1:13-17). As reported in *"Science News"* May 2012, and also in *"Astrophysical Journal,"* the long-awaited results of the "dark matter" experiments had come back, and the invisible matter is still missing. To quote the article, *"This is a major setback to our understanding of the age and formation of the universe*." This was again tested and the results determined that no dark matter shows up in tests designed to detect it according to Tom Siegfried in 2017 in *Science News* magazine.

Current Big Bang models must assume large amounts of what is called "dark matter" and "dark energy" (matter and energy which cannot be identified yet, but is assumed to be there). Up to 95% of the universe is supposedly "dark" according to the current Big Bang theory, therefore, science bases its theories on only 5% of the avail- able evidence. This may be good theory, but it is poor science. Scientific reports in 2018, according to John Hartnett, as a result of ten years of testing, have resulted in dark matter not being a real candidate for what is observed in the universe—bringing science back to square one—no theory works when test results are in.

Other models are out there. Theoretical physicist Moshe Carmeli, in the early 1990's, incorporated Einstein's theory along with the expanding fabric of space itself, to develop a new physics he called "Space Velocity" (an expansion of Einstein's Space-Time). Since 2007, this model has been further expanded by physicist, Dr. John Hartnett, University of Australia. To date, this new physics model predicted the accelerating expansion of the universe two years before observable evidence proved it was accelerating, and it further finds there is no requirement for any "dark matter," or "dark energy" (which no one can identify anyway), which actually is in agreement with Einstein's proofs concerning the solar system and no dark matter. This new physics model actually supports a young universe, based upon gravity. Earth's gravity would produce clocks running slower on earth, in comparison to elapsed time in space, where gravity is much lower. Scientific evidence supports Einstein's theories that time, in space, moves faster than time measured on earth (97, 98).

Gravity is not the only force in space, and electromagnetic fields in space are 10^{40} times more *powerful* than gravity (12). Even using conventional theories, if one uses electromagnetic forces, instead of gravity, to formulate the development of the universe, then the universe we see today could have been originally developed in a period of *hours* instead of billions of years.

The evidence from Hubble space telescope showing that the "oldest" galaxies appear young does not conflict with scientists using paradigm B, because these scientists make no assumptions about age or billions of years. They process observable evidence and derive a theory from that evidence. Scientists using paradigm A, however, are very troubled by the Hubble discoveries because theories of billions of years and clumping processes for galaxy formation are shown to be flawed—evidence points to a young universe.

Scientists, such as Craig Hogan, of the University of Washington, theorize that galaxies were formed by powerful cosmic "brooms," composed of radiation, sweeping particles together. Other scientists speculate that plasma cosmology explains galaxy formation (12). Plasma space, it is theorized, is made up of filaments of electrons and ions, which are twisted together by electromagnetic forces. Again, the parameters of scientists using paradigm A are used in an attempt to explain how scientists could, given up to 200 billion years, in theory, re-create the universe.

A new issue for science emerged in 2019. Dr. Vernon Cupps PhD in Nuclear Physics, is addressing the issue of whether anti-matter should exist in the universe as proposed by theories of Big Bang cosmology by conventional science (paradigm A—old age). Protons and neutrons are in a class of particles known as baryons. An anti-matter baryon is an anti-baryon. If the Big Bang were true, there should be equal amounts of baryons and anti-baryons. But, while matter is everywhere, it is almost impossible to identify any anti-matter. Big Bang theories claim the universe began with some type of quantum fluctuation that expanded as a ball of pure energy and eventually condensed into extremely high-energy electromagnetic waves. These waves then produced equal amounts of baryons and anti-baryons through a process called pair production. When matter and antimatter meet, they produce high energy gamma rays. The problem is that these rays have not been observed. There is no observable evidence. To date (2019), no experimental evidence exists which provides a surplus of matter (which we can clearly see in the cosmos), along with gamma radiation. This leads some to suggest that the Big Bang model is wrong, and another creation model is needed (perhaps paradigm B—young age and creation).

The problem the natural sciences are facing today is that quantum physics, (the physics of matter and sub-atomic particles), and relativity, (the physics of space and time), are not compatible. Mathematically, gravity will not fit into equations in these two areas of physics. The theory is that before the Big Bang, at the point of what is called the "singularity," where the entire universe was a single point, that the four forces (electromagnetic, gravity, strong nuclear force, weak nuclear force), were all in balance, and equal. "Something" caused one of them to be out of balance, and the Big Bang was the result. Gravity's force has become severely weakened somehow, and this is the dilemma for physics trying to prove old age theories.

Particle physicist, John Polkinghorne (Cambridge University), along with Noble Laureate Abdus Salam (Theoretical Physicist, Cambridge University), Brian Josephson (Noble prize in Physics), Nobel Laureate Murray Gell-Mann (research that led to the discovery of the Quark), and physicist Bob Russell, at a series of conferences at Oxford University (as reported in *Discover Science*, in 2011), have raised serious questions as to whether an intelligent designer might be the only explanation for the unexplained aspects of physics today, such as: "*Science cannot identify what mechanism is controlling events in our space/time continuum...the experiments show that space time does not contain all the intelligent entities acting in the world, because something outside of time is coordinating the photons' results...there is strong experimental evidence for accepting that non material beings act in the world.*"

Another new theory, put forth to try to quantify, in natural terms, these areas of physics and gravity, is called superstring. All dimensions of physics, including time, are "*theorized*" to be in the form of vibrating strings of matter, too small to ever be seen. These strings *supposedly* exist in ten or eleven dimensions, according to theories presented in 2009. Superstring is a relatively new theory, and it is already being questioned.

In the April 1993 issue of *Discover*, the work of Syracuse University physicist, Abhay Ashtekar, is discussed. Ashtekar has, over a period of ten years, pieced together four formulas to describe gravity in quantum physics. These form what is described as a "loop space theory," where all space and matter is made of inter-locking rings, too small to ever be seen.

In an article titled: *"Ideas for Time Before the Big Bang,* in the October 2007 issue of *Scientific American*, Gabriele Vaneziano's "Ekpyrosis scenario" to explain what existed before the Big Bang is discussed, where ripples caused by the rebounding universe as it collapses and expands, or bounces from its previous existence, explains the structure of the current universe. This, of course, only makes one ask what was there before the "bouncing" universe.

The outcome of all these approaches, from Einstein, to plasma cosmology, to superstring, to loop space, is that scientists have not been able to prove anything yet. All physics is still in a theoretical state, and one area of physics cannot use its math or theories to work in another area of physics. We are, therefore, asked by sci-entists using paradigm A (old age), to accept various theories as a basis for making assumptions concerning the universe and time. Scientists using paradigm B (young age), limit their research to provable scientific observations. The results are obviously different.

In an article, in the February 1996 issue of *Discover*, Alexander Vilenkin, a physicist at Tufts University in Medford, Massachusetts, provided science with the latest scenario for how this huge universe did the bulk of its expansion, or inflation, as we observe it today, in only a fraction of the very first second of the big bang. Science has *little* argument over the universe expanding. The argument is whether the fraction of a second, in that first instant of expansion, was a trillionth, billionth, or a thousandth of a second.

This time of expansion affects what scientists call the cosmo-logical constant and the Hubble constant. The cosmological con-stant is that density which enables the universe to remain in a static state. A high density would equal a young age for the universe. If the constant number (density) is too big, then the universe expands too fast and pulls us apart. If the number is too low, then gravity won't allow expansion and the universe collapses. Another mea-surement is called the Hubble constant. The Hubble constant is the rate of expansion. A high rate number would equal a fast expansion, and a young age for the universe, whereas, a low number would translate into an older universe.

Most science agrees that the initial major expansion of our universe took less than *one second*, and since 2003, the evidence has been pointing to the universe expanding at an ever-accelerating rate.

Furthermore, the current Big Bang theory also has other problems. These concern the cosmic evolution process, which is the evolving of time, space, and matter. If the universe expansion is too smooth, then matter never clumps, which is needed to form galaxies. If the universe expansion is too rippled, then matter would be pulled back into "black holes," and again, galaxies could not form. No theory has yet been accepted to satisfy the existing evidence. It seems that only a supernatural force (God), can account for what science reports.

The resulting difference between the scientific analysis (using either paradigm A or B), is time. There is plenty of evidence to support a young universe, as scientists using paradigm B are proving.

However, many scientists have adopted paradigm A, because of their need to show enough time for the universe to somehow have been created by entirely natural events, which seem rational and understandable by humans. Of course, this means restricting what evidence is admissible. Only those theories compatible with the views of such scientists are acceptable as working models (or paradigms). Other evidence must be rejected, because if one can't understand it scientifically, it must not be natural, and therefore, not admissible.

Scientists using paradigm B (young age), on the other hand, are not restricted to any requirement to somehow re-create the universe. They may, therefore, freely accept *all* observable data.

The more evidence scientists using paradigm B acquire, the more a young universe and solar system, in the neighborhood of ten thousand years, seems to be the only acceptable answer.

The speed of light and the expansion of the universe are both directly related to what Dr. Gerald Schroder, nuclear physicist, describes as the Quantum Inflation Stretch Factor. The stretch factor is exponential, and points to a very young age for the universe. It seems light traveled at much higher speeds when the universe first began inflating, and therefore, what we today perceive as a universe billions of years old, may have developed in a matter of hours, and not years, because we are in fact observing slower speeds of expansion today.

In the 1880's, it was verified by science that the speed of light is not a constant—it slows down when it passes through water.

Scientists using paradigm B, point to actual observations by Russian astrophysicist, V. S. Troitski (2), and Barry Setterfield and Trevor Norman, Mathematics Department, Flinders University, Australia (3), which indicate the speed of light has been slowing down at an exponential rate, ever since that very first second the entire universe came into being. This would additionally change decay rates of radio isotopes, and further verify a young earth age.

This is additionally supported by scientist, T. C. Van Flandern (4), who reported that twenty-six years of actual observations suggest that atomic clocks are also slowing down.

The principle of the speed of light always being constant, is under further attack from physicists, including Dr. Lijun Wang at the NEC Institute at Princeton, who has indicated that light pulses can accelerate up to 300 times faster than the normal velocity of light. Also, physicists at the Italian National Research Council have transmitted microwaves twenty-five percent faster than light. In April of 2005, at Warwick University, at a physics conference, several scientists reported that the speed of light may actually be slowing down.

The red shift of distant galaxies has been theorized as the explanation of how great the distance is to galaxies, and theoretically, how to measure their rate of recession away from us. The theory is, the redder the shift, the greater the recession speed, which translates into greater distance and long time periods for light to travel to us. These red frequencies of light, however, are not evenly spread through the spectrum of red light. In fact, evidence shows the red frequencies are distributed in multiples, or a quantum step arrangement. Quantum physics measures and describes this phenomena. The frequency of light changes or jumps to the next quantum or resonant level of frequency, instead of gradually changing frequency. This means there are millions of light years between one group of galaxies and the next red shifted group of galaxies, and so on to other groups of galaxies. In other words, there are many "layers" of galaxies, separated by vast stretches of time and space.

In 2019, Physicist Russell Humphreys has reported that studies concerning these patterns of red shifted galaxies show that they are all concentric and centered on our own galaxy—meaning we appear to be at the center of it all. The odds of our being at this unique place in the universe is a trillion to one—meaning that it could not happen naturally—there must be another explanation.

The current Big Bang model continues to be a problem for scientists as more information is gathered by satellites. Dr. John Hartnett, physicist, University of Australia, summarizes some of the problems with the current Big Bang theory, in his book *Starlight, Time, and the New Physics*. The first problem concerns the "Red

Shift patterns of galaxies." Current Big Bang models *assume* the expanding universe is "homogeneous" (all matter is located on the expanding shell or sphere – like dots on a balloon), and thus, there is no center to the universe. In this current Big Bang model, no matter where you are at on the expanding sphere, the universe appears to be expanding. However, evidence from Red Shift patterns from the Hubble Space Telescope in 2004 actually supports an "isotropic" universe (where matter is spread throughout space in *all directions* – including the entire volume of the sphere of the expanding universe, not just the outer shell). Hubble space telescope evidence shows that the "Red Shift" is quantized in spheres of one hundred million light years. The galaxies are dispersed in spheres, with little in between, and we, here on earth, appear to be within one million light years of the actual center of these rings, or spheres. The Big Bang theory accounts for only one sphere, and no center. Obviously, the evidence doesn't match the current Big Bang theory.

Another problem is the "Horizon problem." Even though points in the universe are separated by billions of light years, they are all at the same temperature. This is a problem, because in order for temperatures to be equal, diverse regions of space must share radiation between all points in space—and these points are too far apart for radiation to travel to, even at the speed of light (meaning that at a relative recent point in time, all points of the universe had to be close enough so as to share common source of radiation)... This points to a young universe. If the universe is truly 13.5 billion years old, the farthest points would have a greater variation in temperatures than evidence supports.

Stars described as "red giants" will eventually turn into "white dwarfs. These were once thought to take large amounts of time to transition. However, the star Ceres is a white dwarf today, and was a red giant less than 2,000 years ago. This evidence means distance and time to the galaxies in space cannot be measured by this red pattern, because this red pattern of light does not represent time and distance, but instead, the red pattern of frequencies represents quantum steps of radiometric energy. The higher the frequency, the higher the energy state, and these frequencies occur in quantum steps.

It seems, as the universe ages, that the expansion of matter in space speeds up. The energy of electromagnetic waves at zero degrees Celsius, (Z P E, zero point energy, which is the energy that keeps the atomic structure from collapsing), is required in less and less quantities in the expansion. As frequencies stretch to a lower energy level, and matter continues expanding and becomes less dense, a point is reached where there is enough surplus Z P E to allow the frequency to jump or increase to a higher quantum energy state (or frequency rate), thus, explaining why the universe is expanding at an increased rate.

Conventional scientists theorize that it would take 15 billion to 200 billion years to form our solar system, through a process called "clumping," where matter condenses into stars.

Concerning the theory that over long periods of time, star-forming clouds of matter condensed, giving us galaxies, stars and planets, a report has been issued by NASA's Ames Research Center scientists Louis Allamandola, Scott Sandford, Dutch scientist Xander Tielens, and German astronomer Tom M. Herbst, in the November 1992 issue of *Astrophysical Journal*. In the report, the scientists have identified two types of clouds that always remain separated, one of which has billions of tons of diamond molecules. Because these clouds cannot merge or cluster, this provides evidence that clumping theories are flawed. The report says revisions will be needed in current theories that hold that over long stretches of time, the star-forming clouds condense, to give birth to stars. Scientist Sandford is quoted as saying: "It means that all our models of galaxy evolution are flawed."

The Hubble space telescope proved that the "star nurseries," (pictured in school textbooks), cannot be proven as sources for newly-forming stars. Stars cannot form from the "condensing gas," because scientists tell us that heat forms from any condensing action, and actually causes the gas to expand. Evidence from measuring gas clouds in space, shows expansion of the gas clouds *in all cases*, not contraction, according to Dr. Jason Lisle, Ph.D. Astrophysics, University of Colorado. Still, these "Star Nursery" pictures are taught to our students in government schools…which are required to ignore God.

In 2015, this gas expansion (not contraction), was again explained by astrophysicist Jason Lisle—"Gas is very resistant to being compressed…in a typical nebula, the gas pressure far exceeds the minuscule force of gravity." In 2019, this continues to be the debate—conventional science requires "dark energy" and "dark matter" (discussed earlier) to theoretically make stars form. And, still, as of 2019, none has been identified—only theories.

Many theories were developed as the result of the Hubble space program, which has discovered that at the center of *every* galaxy, there is a black hole. The latest version of how stars and galaxies could have formed is as follows: following the Big Bang, billions of dense black holes were created, which consumed most matter close to them. At a certain point in time (suggested to be 13.5 billion years ago), stars began forming from the condensing matter still left around the black hole. These stars then began circulating around the black holes forming the galaxies. It is conceded by scientists that all galaxies seemed to have formed at the same time in cosmic history. The difference between this conventional science and the Bible is still "age"—recent (young), or billions of years ago.

Additionally, a new theory of how stars form, called "Triggered Star Formation," has been put forward by Xavier Koenig of the Harvard-Smithsonian Center for astrophysics, as reported in *Science Illustrated Magazine*. The theory goes as follows: *First*, a massive star forms (already I see a problem), which then causes radiation to push outward, and force outside matter to condense into newer stars, and these newer stars, once formed, also generate radiation to push still further outward, and force farther away matter to condense, forming even more stars, and so on.

At the present time, there is no real evidence for how galaxies and stars formed. There is only theory. Furthermore, these theories state that at least one new star forms each year to make up for stars, which theories assume, have died over these millions of years. However, no one has ever witnessed a star turn on, which points to a very young cosmos.

Scheffler and Elsasser, in their book *Physics of the Galaxy and Interstellar Matter,* report on rotational patterns of the galaxies. Galaxies with twisted spiral arms are evidence of a young galaxy. If a galaxy were very old, it would look more like a featureless smear of stars, due to the differing rotational speeds of the stars, within each galaxy. Ironically, galaxies in the universe (even those supposedly extremely old), *all* show evidence of twisted spirals, and therefore, a young age.

Our own galaxy is a spiral, and if it is even 10 billion years old, as estimated by scientists using the paradigm A criteria, then our galaxy should be a smear and no longer be a spiral, but it is, which points to a young age. Reinhard Ghez, from the Max Planck Institute of Physics in Germany, in a report in *Astronomy*, February 2008, states that while doing studies using the Keck Telescope, he measured the spectrum of stars at the center of our galaxy, and determined that the evidence shows our galaxy must be less than six million (not billion) years old, or less. Science tells us that stars cannot form in galaxy core regions of intense magnetic fields and strong gravitational forces, and yet, the evidence discovered points to all these stars being very young.

In 2008, the Hubble Space Telescope team announced that they have a new record for the oldest galaxy. This galaxy is nearly as old as the "Big Bang" itself, and yet appears to have formed quickly. *Science Daily.com* quoted a team member; "*We certainly were surprised to find such a bright young galaxy 13 billion years in the past.*" The current theory for a time frame for the beginning of the universe is 13.5 billion years ago, according to conventional science, however, discoveries like these, challenge the conventional understanding.

Science Illustrated Magazine, August 2008, pages 58-60, discussed the latest problem for the "big bang" theory. Both the WMAP Satellite (Wilkinson Microwave Anisotropy Probe), and the Radio Telescope in the Very Large Array in New Mexico, have confirmed that a very large cold spot, or void, has been discovered in the universe, which does not match up with current theories of how the "Big Bang" created the universe. Astronomer Lawrence Rudnic, and a team of astronomers at the University of Minnesota, are examining the data. Current theory is that the initial expansion of the universe immediately after the "Big Bang" would have evenly distributed matter throughout the cosmos. This is a fundamental principle of the "Big Bang" called the Cosmological Principle. Rudnic said: *"Scientists will need to re-evaluate what processes led to the development of structure in the universe."* The void makes it necessary to explore new theories about the way the universe formed.

David F. Coppedge of the Cassini program at the Jet Propulsion Laboratory in an article on globular clusters, noted that these can no longer be thought of as collections of ancient stars. Globular clusters appear to us as millions of stars packed into a small angle of space. It turns out that the scientists (and the current textbooks being used) are wrong, as the consensus (up until now), was that these clusters comprised the oldest objects in the universe. However, Hubble Space Telescope, and others, have now confirmed that these theories are all flawed. These clusters contain a mixed population of stars, and even some planets, which means that the previous theories of star formation, galaxy formation, and age, are all flawed.

Big Bang theory suggests that all the elements we have were generated during star formation, and star death, as the universe has aged. However, this is only a theory. Actual scientific evidence cannot explain the existence of any elements from fusion beyond the basic element of iron.

More supporting evidence of a young universe is presented by Harold S. Slusher (5), and Wayne M. Zage (7), based on observations of twenty-seven binary star systems. Their data suggests that light in deep space travels in curved paths on "Riemannian surfaces." This hyperbolic geometry of space would mean light from the farthest reaches of the universe would reach the earth in only 15.71 years.

Scientists who theorize about long time periods, suggest it would theoretically take about 10 billion to 200 billion years for the solar system to develop, and an additional 4.5 billion more years for the earth and moon to develop, and life to evolve to its present form. However, no one has ever observed a galaxy forming, a solar system forming, or even a sun forming. It is only *theory* that suggests it must take billions of years.

As of 2019, concerning the creation of our solar system, science has discovered that our solar system is unique in the cosmos. All other 2,600 solar systems discovered show planets circling their sun at very close orbits—closer than even Mercury in our system. This causes science to question our current theories of planet formation.

The problem in understanding how our system could have evolved is that formation theories require that the space debris which would form the planets and moons needs to spin in agreement with the sun. But, our system shows a 6 degree tilt, which points to a distant planet (as yet undiscovered) needed to account for this tilt. In other words, our system should not exist as it does—it is unique!

Furthermore, the earth is slowing down every year. Scientists know the earth rotated much faster in the past, and if the solar system is millions of years old (not even one billion), then the wind speeds would have been in excess of 5,000 miles per hour, which would have caused any water on the surface to escape, whereas, if the planet is only tens of thousands of years old, the rotational speed would not be a factor.

Relative to dynamic time (up until 1967), the physical orbit of the solar system was used to track time. Now however, atomic clocks are compared with atomic rates. This is a bad scientific comparison, as they are related to a common source. Currently, every year or two, we must add leap seconds to adjust for the slowing down of the earth's rotation.

Observations pointed out by scientists using paradigm B, of the relationship of the moon and earth, show evidence of a very young solar system. Lord Kelvin calculated the rate of decay of the earth's rotation and determined the age of the earth to be very young (8).

Dr. Louis B. Slichter, Professor of Geophysics, Massachusetts Institute of Technology (9), acknowledges the time scale of the earth-moon system presents a major problem to the acceptance of a theory of even 1 billion years, much less 4.5 billion years, for earth-moon formation. Dr. Thomas Barnes, Professor of Physics, University of Texas, El Paso, has calculated the speed of recession of the moon from the earth, using the Roche Limit (2.44 times the radius of the larger body, which is the closest distance two objects can be to each other without one of them breaking apart), and has shown that the moon would have to be much farther away from the earth, if the age of the solar system is even a fraction of that theorized by scientists using paradigm A and old age (10). Calculations show that only 1.5 *million* years ago (not billions), the moon would have been so close to the earth, that it would have caused tidal effects nine times greater than those today.

Science is still struggling with the evidence of "angular momentum," and how this evidence does not support the theories of how the solar system was formed 4.5 billion years ago. The theory is that all the planets in the solar system should be rotating the same way, because they all were supposedly formed from a common source in cosmic evolution (a major collision of stars, or an explosion of a star). However, two of the planets (Venus and Uranus), spin in the opposite direction, and also, six moons spin in the opposite direction from what the theory predicts. And, in fact, our own moon has a different element makeup than our earth, again indicating the theory of a common source is flawed.

In 2014, James Gaier, physicist at NASA's Glenn Research Center reported evidence showing dust accumulations of 1 millimeter per 1,000 years—meaning if the Earth-Moon system were 4.5 billion years old, there should be over 1,000 inches of dust on the moon. This is only theory however, as the landing on the moon showed almost no dust, which is what the conventional scientists predicted. Perhaps this evidence of little dust does show a young moon, but there are reasonable arguments as to why little dust should be found even after billions of years. The jury is still out on this one.

Concerning planets, Saturn is losing its rings. Science tells us these rings should be already gone if the solar system is three to four billion years old. In 2019 David Catchpoole reported on questions surrounding what the rings of Saturn are actually composed of—mostly of water ice, whereas Neptune's and Uranus' rings are mostly rock. Science reports that Saturn's rings are made of very clean water, which cannot be explained if the rings are billions of years old—they would have to be polluted by dust and debris according to SETI institute Matthew Tiscareno. Also, the heat generated from planets and the moon (as measured by the space satellite project), indicate that the solar system should be young, as the heat levels are still very high. Dr. Jason Lisle, Ph.D. in astrophysics at the University of Colorado, states that NASA satellites have measured the temperature being emitted from Jupiter and Neptune, and determined they are still very hot—Too hot to be billions of years old, as theorized by conventional science (Paradigm A).

All these observations are consistent with a young universe, galaxies, and solar system, forming right after that first split-second of expansion in which the COBE satellite data points.

Concerning the planet Mars, scientists are trying to determine how it formed because its material make-up is so different from the other planets close to it. Both the make-up of Mars and the Earth's moon suggests they came from somewhere else...not from the space debris which formed Earth and Jupiter. In 2017, planetary scientist Kevin Walsh, and geologist Stephen Mojzsis suggest that early in the solar systems formation Jupiter must have caused objects like Mars to dislodge from their orbits (which were further out), to where they are now. The theory is Mars, and perhaps even the moon, may have been originally located around the asteroid belt, and this could account for their unusual make-up.

Evidence for a young age for the sun keeps growing, as science gathers more information. In 1976, Russian astronomers were able to measure the global oscillations of the sun (86). Science has determined that if a star is young, it will not yet possess a dense core to support nuclear reactions. The energy the young sun generates comes from the gravitational contraction it is going through, until millions of years have passed to allow a dense core to develop. The Russian team found our sun to still be very young. This was confirmed by a British team also (87).

Concerning supernovas, these happen because fusion within a star ends, and gravity causes an implosion, which then causes gases to explode outwards. Supernovas are categorized into three classes, or three stages.

Stage 1: A supernova which is under 2,000 years old. Science has identified five of these.

Stage 2: Supernovas theorized to be up to 10 million years old (not billion). Science has identified 200 of these.

Stage 3: Supernovas theorized to be over 10 million years old. Ironically, science cannot find any – **zero**. Theoretically, if the universe is 14 billion years old, science says there should be over 5,000 identified, but none have been found.

Gas clouds emitted by collapsing stars called "Planetary Nebulae" (also known as "butterfly" or "hourglass" nebulae), are all thought to be less than 10,000 years old, even by conventional science.

Further evidence supporting unconventional science (paradigm B), and a young age for the solar system, comes from John A. Eddy, Harvard Smithsonian Center for Astrophysics, in Boulder, Colorado, and Aram A. Boornazian, Mathematician, S. Ross and Co, Boston, Massachusetts (11). The data they put together provided evidence of the sun's shrinkage rate of 0.1 percent per century, which rules out any possibility of the earth being very old, as theorized by conventional scientists. If the sun was only a few thousand years old, extrapolating backwards at the rate of 0.1 percent per century, then the sun's size a few thousand years ago would not have been so large as to engulf the earth. However, if the sun were as old as 700,000 years, much less than the 4.5 billion some theorize, then, the sun's size would have been so large that it would have consumed the earth, and several other planets as well.

Theories vary from the sun's brightness, in the first billion years being forty percent less bright than today, to only sixteen percent less brightness than today. A less bright sun means life would need to form under colder conditions, which means there would be a need in the past for greenhouse gases, such as methane and ammonia, which are toxic. In order to have temperatures needed for life to evolve. 3.5 billion years ago, when science believes life began to evolve in liquid soup, the temperature of the surface is estimated to have dropped to 27 degrees below freezing, obviously a problem for science needing billions of years for evolution.

This problem for the conventional scientists is further complicated by the long-standing dilemma scientists call a "Low Neutrino Flux" (88). This low flux measurement points to little or no nuclear activity in the sun's core. Again, pointing to a young age for the sun.

Processes within the sun are not fully known by science. Some scientist say nuclear fusion is underway now, and some say only gravitational factors are in effect.

More recently, scientists measuring the levels of lithium and beryllium (89) discovered that the sun has almost no lithium, which would be consumed in about 7,500 years at a temperature of three million degrees. But, the levels of beryllium, which would be destroyed at temperatures above four million degrees, appear to be abundant. Therefore, the sun's temperature is below four million degrees and still quite young. If the sun were billions of years old, its temperatures would have to be at least 15 million degrees with a dense core and heavy nuclear activity. The sun would appear from all this evidence to be very young.

In the Bible, in Revelation 16:8-9, Isaiah 30:26, and Malachi 4:1, we read that the earth will end by being scorched with great fire. In Joel 2:30-31, Matthew 24:29, and Isaiah 13:9-13, we read that the earth will be dark and cold in the end of days. How can both of these scenarios be true? The answer lies in what astronomers refer to as a nova. The sun first goes extremely hot for seven to ten days, and then goes dark. Dr. Josef S. Shidovsky of the Shtenberg State Astronomical Institute of Moscow, reports that when the sun's hydrogen supply drops to forty-nine percent, and the helium content increases to fifty-one percent, our sun will go nova.

Scientists also tell us that our sun should last a long time, because its' hydrogen supply is only about *half* gone. *Think about it!*

Also, a gamma ray burst, which is very deadly, is capable of doing the same thing as a nova, scorching with bright light, and then going dark.

Actual evidence supports a very young universe and solar system. As COBE satellite evidence shows, the universe did the bulk of its expansion in one-thousandth of one second. If electromagnetic forces are substituted in the calculations for the weak force of gravity in space (12), then the galaxies and the solar system could have formed in a matter of hours and days.

Still more evidence supports paradigm B and young age, through measurements of escape velocities of stars from star clusters. Clusters are groups of stars, much smaller than galaxies. The high velocity of the components stars are overcoming the self-gravitation of the cluster, and causing the clusters to break up. Harold S. Slusher, in his manuscript, *"Age of the Earth from some Astronomical Indicators"* says: "The stars are diverging from a common point so fast that in some cases, if their motion were projected backwards to this common point, the cluster could have originated only several thousand years ago."

Concerning comets, Lyttleton (56), has estimated the maximum life of short-period comets to be only 10,000 years, and the life period of a long-term comet could not exceed 100,000 years, which again, points to a young universe.

The theory of conventional science is that comets come out of a distant "Oort Cloud". This theorized cloud is thought to be 50 Au away (Astronomical units – a unit is equal to the distance from the sun to our earth – 93,000,000 miles). But no evidence exists of this "cloud." Pluto is 39 Au away. A new theory in 2005 suggests that the Kuiper Belt (the ring of objects outside the orbit of

Neptune, which includes Pluto), is very broad, including the Oort Cloud area up to 50 Au away. The objects that have been identified in this Kuiper Belt area are not the same as comets, and do not become comets. But, science is at a loss to explain exactly where the comets originate from, so this area seems plausible.

There is, of course, no evidence that this is where the comets come from, but if the solar system is older than 10 to 20,000 years old, then there must be a "source" for all these comets still in existence today. Unfortunately, no evidence of any of these areas of comet formation can be given. All these points of origin are based on speculation. The only evidence that science can point to, is that comets last for only about 10,000 years, and there are still some around, so the solar system must be at least several thousand years old, but beyond that we can only speculate as to old ages.

There is no evidence from these areas that the solar system is billions of years old.

NASA initially reported that rocks brought back from the moon tested from two to eight billion years old. However, scientists at Rice University, Department of Geology and Space Science, said that the rare gases found in the rocks used for dating did not come from radiogenic sources, but from a solar wind, during a period of one to two thousand years ago. Also, it has been noted that the moon rocks were glazed. In order for moon rocks to have become glazed, the Rice scientists stated that they would have had to have been heated to a temperature of 1,000-1,300 degrees centigrade. It is known that potassium vaporizes at 744 degrees centigrade, so that if one uses the potassium-argon technique of dating, it would be worthless. Yet, this is the method NASA used to date the moon rocks. Scientists at Rice University and other well- known scientists such as Dr. Melvin Cook, Nobel Prize medalist, say that their analysis indicates the moon rocks are perhaps, at the oldest, 10,000 years of age.

In 2013-2014, scientists at University of Michigan reported large quantities of water detected in moon rocks which should not be there if the moon is 4.5 billion years old. Planetary scientist Paul Lucey said he was "completely blown away" by the reports, and many scientists acknowledge that no known mechanism can account for the water in these moon rocks—whether from the surface or the interior, it isn't possible.

Further, Dr. Cook (57), points to the age of the moon in the order of thousands of years, not millions or billions, based upon levels of helium-4 measured on the moon. Additionally, measurements of helium on the earth, by Dr. Cook (58), and Dr. Faul (59), show that accumulation of helium, which enters our atmosphere from the solar wind and radioactive decay of uranium rock, show the earth to be about 10,000 years old.

These questions about the moon brought up even more questions concerning the earth and its origins. Where did all the water on the earth come from? The quantity of water on earth is impossible to account for from icy comets and other space sources. As of 2019 there is still no known source for earth's water, or the moons for that matter.

Scientists using paradigm A, must ignore all this data, as it does not fit the theory of long periods of time. Scientists using paradigm B, are not restricted to only theories of vast ages, but are able to explore *all* evidence, which ironically leads to acceptance of a young age of 10,000 to 15,000 years for the universe.

Given enough time, anything is possible. This is a concept humans can handle. Even though the concept of billions of years is only a theory, it somehow seems believable.

Evidence seems to support an age of only thousands of years, and yet, this seems somehow unreal to conventional scientists.

The current conventional scientific explanation to answer the age-old question of: "What happened before the Big Bang?" was addressed in *Astronomy* magazine, in May 1996. The article quotes the November 1994 article in *Scientific American* by Andrei Linde, of Stanford University, and also Nobel laureate, Steve Weinberg: *"There wasn't a beginning....There is a constant genesis, or boiling of universes, in an ocean of cosmic nothing or Nirvana."* This newest scientific theory seems to require a lot of faith, and little evidence.

AGE AND GEOLOGY

See *Target Truth Ministries.com*
for <u>News & Updates</u>

I t is important to know all about rocks, because evolutionists theorize that our ancestors were, at one time, rocks. The term "pet rock" takes on real meaning, if one believes that "once upon a time" we were all rocks, and we evolved from the minerals of rocks.

Rocks come in three basic forms. Igneous rocks are from volcanoes, and contain dating material, but *no* fossils. Metamorphic rocks are surface rocks, subject to high temperatures. Sedimentary rocks are water deposits and form through a "cementing" process of pressure compaction. These rocks contain fossils, but *no* dating material.

The geologic column one sees in a college textbook only occurs in one place in the world. That place is in the textbook. The geologic column of strata of rocks were actually identified and classified in the 1800's, before fossils were identified, and long before radiometric dating methods were developed. Ten basic types or strata were identified to be used as a general guide, in order to make reference to systems and types of rock—not to age. These systems are not uniform and appear different in various parts of the earth. The geologists who developed the system of identifying the various strata theorized that a catastrophic process, several thousand years ago, caused various types of rocks and strata to appear inverted, repeated, or even inserted, and therefore, not conforming to any general system of strata. In fact, reports in 2016 state data from continents and ocean basins now show that the ten types of strata are actually very poorly represented on a global scale—about seventy-seven percent of the earth's surface area on land, and under the sea, have *7 or more strata,* or seventy percent of the strata types, entirely missing (13). In other words, these layer's names actually represent types of rock, not age.

Studies reported to the French Academy of Science, and the European Congress of Sedimentology in 1995 provide proof that strata which run horizontal are actually deposited by a vertical process. This is true of both coastal areas and deep seas. During periods of great flooding, the horizontal layers are laid down from top to bottom (vertically), as the water flows (horizontally). Studies of Mount St. Helens showed that in one day, 600 feet of various different strata were laid down in this way.

The volcanic eruption of Mount St. Helens, in Washington State, showed that dense and light compaction layers do form on top of each other as a result of flooding. For much of the last century, scientists would not accept this fact, but the evidence is clear now.

Early geologists used paradigm B (young age), which requires facts to be observed. Conventional scientists, who felt they had to be able, in theory anyway, to re-create the earth and various rock strata, were forced to adopt paradigm A, and a theory of billions of years needed to accomplish a layer-by-layer sedimentary build up. This, despite the fact that seventy percent of the earth's surface is missing seventy percent of these different strata layers.

In order to attach *age* to the rocks and various layers, several methods have been tried. The rocks, themselves, are subjected to a process of radiometric dating, and fossils, found in the rocks, can be put through a carbon-14 process and other dating methods (as is discussed in the next section). Scientists using paradigm A theorize that the layers of rock were formed over billions of years by sediment layers slowly piling up, and these layers were eventually broken up by flooding, vulcanization, and other catastrophic events. Actual evidence from reports in 2016 show there are no erosion marks between many of these layers, which suggests very short time periods between layers—just the opposite of scientists who theorize long periods of sediment build up. In fact, the separation breaks between layers has now been identified as being formed when these differing layers dry out—a difficult fact to overcome for those who look for long periods between layers, which should show erosion.

One of the areas which still stump scientists today is how granite was formed. If scientists melt down granite, it does not reform back into granite. Furthermore, polonium halos, which are found in granite, actually only form in a "cool" state, and they form in a matter of minutes. All of this means that granite probably formed quickly, and in a cool state. There is no scientific theory which can explain this, unless, of course, granite was "created." (see Ice section).

Carbon-14 and other radiometric dating methods have all proven fallible as dating techniques (as is discussed in the next section). Additionally, fossils and rocks so dated in one "era," are often found in different strata layers of supposedly different ages (18). In fact, there is *often* little relationship between strata and speculated "age" (14), which effectively defeats old-age theories based on sedimentary layers.

Scientists, using either paradigm A or B, basically agree that catastrophic events, vulcanization, glacier ice, meteors, and massive flooding, have given us our present mixture of strata, *often* with layers missing (seventy percent), mixed, repeated, and inverted. Scientists, however, differ on time and age. Scientists using paradigm A insist upon science, at least theoretically, being able to re-create these deposits and layers, mixed as they are. This, according to paradigm A and old age, required an estimated 4.5 billion years of slow sedimentary build-up. Additionally, because so much time is theoretically involved, catastrophic events presumably occurred at different periods over those 4.5 billion years. Some scientists even require more than one ice age.

Stalactites and stalagmites are theorized to have been formed by water dripping over millions of years. Yet, in many caves, bats which have died, were buried before their bodies could decay, indicating rapid burial, not millions of years.

Scientists estimate that at the current erosion rates, all the mountains would be flat in fourteen million years. Yet, the mountain ranges actually show signs of little erosion, indicating a recent formation.

The percentage of minerals and salts in the ocean is 3.6%, and at the current rate of deposits of minerals and salts to the ocean, it is estimated that this level of salts and minerals (3.6%), would only take 5,000 years to form, not millions or billions of years, even if in the beginning, there were no salts or minerals to begin with.

Scientists have measured the amounts of deposits which flow into the Mississippi basin, and have concluded that the Gulf of Mexico should have filled up long ago, in only 30,000 years. Because the gulf is far from being full, the conclusion is that the earth cannot be billions of years old.

Scientists have measured the amount of helium in the atmosphere and determined that even if there was no helium present in the beginning, it would take only 2 million years for the present helium levels to accumulate, not the 4.5 billion years which is estimated by evolution for the age of the earth.

Scientists have analyzed sand dunes and discovered that, in as little as five years, a sand dune deposit can be glazed or frosted, and turned into solid sandstone, if dry winds are available after a flood. However, some in conventional science estimate that the Sahara Desert has been developing over a period of about 4,000-5,000 years. Still others in conventional science report evidence that the Sahara Desert, as well as Death Valley in America, were once flooded and experienced great rainfall for a long period of time. The issue is always age—when did it happen?

Because conventional scientists using paradigm A theorize about billions of years being needed to form various layers, they therefore, assign *ages* to fossils found in these layers, even though the same fossil types are often found in other theoretical *age* layers, as well. A major source of fossils is found in the Cambrian layer. Ironically, scientists can't explain why life appears suddenly in the fossil record in this layer, fully developed, fully varied, with *no* links between species (60, 61,74).

Science bases its theories of "ages for strata" upon using *only* the vertebrate fossils as evidence. These vertebrate fossils account for only .000125% of all fossils, which means that science is basing its theories on less than one percent of the available evidence, and that is poor science. Additionally, vertebrate life forms are very mobile and can escape catastrophes (like a flood), easier than non-vertebrate life.

Dr. Aaron Judkins notes in the book *"Evolution and Human Fossil Footprints"* that when vertebrate fossils are not available, then so-called "index" fossils (invertebrate) are used to date the rock layer. Dr. Herbert PhD., noted in 2016 that records document that the use of circular reasoning is used to support theories of evolution by using rocks to date fossils (when convenient), and fossils to date rocks (when convenient).

Furthermore, as discussed in the previous pages, because strata are laid down from top to bottom (vertically), in a horizontal direction (sometimes hundreds of feet of layers), fossils found in these strata, therefore, often reflect the same age whether in the top, or bottom layer. In fact, the fossils on the top layers are actually deposited before those fossils on the bottom layer, due to this horizontal direction of the movement of water.

Scientists using paradigm B and young age, on the other hand, observe that the geologic column and strata mixture is explainable by catastrophic phenomena, except that there is no evidence that billions of years are needed. Examples of the layers of the Grand Canyon from the limestone (15), to the calcite muds, and re-crystallization (16), are explained by rapid formation, as opposed to millions of years. Mount St. Helens teaches us that the stratified layers, commonly characterizing geological formations, can form very rapidly by flow processes. On June 12, 1980, a deposit, 25 feet thick, with sedimentary laminae and bed, formed in *one* day, and a mudflow from Mount St. Helens on March 19, 1982, eroded a canyon system up to 140 feet deep. In fact, between 1980 and 1985, up to 600 feet of thickness of strata formed (17). Geologists now agree that the lowest layer of the Grand Canyon (which covers several states of the United States), was deposited by fluid dynamics (a flood). Further, it is estimated by scientists that this mud flow traveled at about 90 miles per hour to create the deposits in the Grand Canyon. The evidence for this understanding of fluid dynamics came from the deposits laid down during the flooding after Mount St. Helens.

In 2018-2019, Brian Thomas, MS Biotechnology reported that studies show conclusively that a flood, as described in Genesis where water rises for months, and then is surging back and forth for months, and then falling, eroding, and redepositing all the while, is exactly what we see evidence of in today's water laid rock layers. Geologic anomalies like inselbergs such as Ayers Rock in Australia and Spitzkoppe Rock in Namibia, are examples of erosion caused by a massive flood, and do not need millions of years of erosion to form them. Also, formations of natural bridges like Sipapu, and Landscape Arch, Delicate Arch, and Wall Arch, all in Utah, as well as the landscape of Provadia Bulgaria where the rocks on the *top* of the plateau contain marine shells, are all examples of a massive flood, and do not require millions of years to form.

A very large graveyard of Ichthyosaurs (about fifty complete fossils), have been discovered in Chile, pointing to a massive land burial caused by a flood preserving them. Conventional science estimates their age at 130-140 million years. However, some of the bones being removed actually have some soft tissue still attached to the bones (see later chapter on Dinosaurs and soft tissue). Other dinosaur fossils also suggest burial by sudden massive flood. In 2019, in Mexico, discoveries of remains of Duck-Billed dinosaur, a Tyrannosaurs, and a Triceratops, all point to sudden burial in the Cerro del Pueblo formation. This formation of rock is extremely thick pointing to massive flood burial, as opposed to slow sediment burial.

Flood legends exist from all over the world including the American Indians, the Fijians, the Hawaiians, the Eskimos, the Australian Aborigines, the Babylonians, and the Chinese. In fact, archaeologist uncovered human remains of masses of people scientifically shown to have been buried in a flood dating to about 2,000 B.C. in China at the Yellow River Valley site, as reported in 2016 in *Science News*. People isolated from world cultures, such as the Biami people of Papua New Guinea, have a great flood story in their history. So, too, the people of the Andaman Islands, who believe their ancestors survived a great flood in a boat after their god Puluga found them to be disobedient. The Choctaw Tribe of America have a flood story of how the Great Spirit was grieved as the people became wicked, and he told one man, Oklatabashih, to collect animals and build a boat and take his family on board the boat. The boat floated for many moons until Okaltabashih sent a dove out which returned with grass in its beak. In Brazil, in the 16th Century, Frenchman Andre Thevet told the story of the Cape Frio Indians, where two brothers who were opposites (Cain and Able?), survived a great flood that covered the whole earth, with their wives by climbing two tall trees. The famous Aztec Calendar (1479 A.D.), records a great flood that destroyed mankind.

It is interesting that all the world's deltas, which are formed by the rivers dumping into them, all seem to have a similar "age." Dr. David Livingston reports that scientists estimate all deltas around the world date to about 3,000 B.C., which would point to the beginning of rivers flowing at that same time—meaning that something like a great flood re-set all rivers and their deltas worldwide.

The Hawaiian Islands are presumed to be millions of years old. However, according to research by Tim Clarey PhD., the evidence that the Islands are in fact very young comes from the erosion rates which science can measure. If the Islands were millions of years old, then they should have eroded away long ago. But, if the Islands were only 4,500 years old, and created during a great earth eruption and flood, then they would have experienced an erosion rate resulting in about one-third of a mile—and that is exactly what science finds.

The glaciers and ice formations also have scientists divided into *age* arguments and, of course, there are those who argue that the only theories that should be acceptable to science are those that can, in concept anyway, be re-created by scientists. The paradigm A scientist, therefore, suggests an earth that is billions of years old, with several ice *ages,* and very old ice formations. However, actual observations made have supported the paradigm B example of a young earth age. At the northern tip of the Greenland Ice Sheets, Camp Century, ice is measured to a depth of 4,000 feet and has been calculated to be only 6,000 years old, after accounting for compaction, precipitation rates, the number of annual oscillations of oxygen isotopes, and the number of layers showing high particulate levels at periods of volcanic activity, which have been historically correlated to eruptions from as far back as 553 A.D. (19).

Scientists, using paradigm A, point to core samples taken from the 12,000 foot-thick Antarctic ice flows, as examples of very old ice formations. But oxygen isotopes cannot verify the old age that they theorized. Further, these theories of old age are based on accepting today's snowfall rates, as the typical rates for thousands of years (20). Scientists from both paradigm A and B, however, agree that great flooding and catastrophic events took place before the recent ice age. These events would have greatly increased precipitation rates at the lowest levels. These higher precipitation rates, to scientists using the paradigm B method, correlate to a young Antarctic ice sheet, and easily explain the thickness of 12,000 feet.

Scientists using paradigm A theories suggest there was more than one ice age, covering millions of years. Scientists using paradigm B, however, point out that Pleistocene fossils are rare in glaciated areas, which is mysterious, if there were many interglacials. Practically all the mega faunal extinctions were after the *last* ice formation, a difficult problem, if there was more than one ice age (21).

According to A.D. Watt in *"From Eden to the Moon,"* the polar regions were free of ice until the Ice Age began a few hundred years "after" the great flood around the world. Geologic studies indicate that both polar ice caps appear to have started at the same time. A.D. Watt in *"Secrets of the Polar Ice,"* states that many are convinced the ice receded in hundreds of years, not tens of thousands. Thermal analysis, in comparison with the ice cores from the polar caps, indicate that the ice age extended from about 2,000 B.C. to 1,000 B.C. (101—pgs. 74-79).

At the 1992 annual meeting of the American Geophysical Union, scientists, many of whom have been puzzled by theories of the occurrences of ice ages during times when the earth was supposedly warm, presented evidence rejecting all theories of multiple ice ages carving out the earth's surface. These new theories of land formation are based upon research by Verne Overbeck, John Marshall, and Hans Aggarwal, at the NASA Ames Research

Center, in Mountain View, California, showing that tillite deposits, usually attributed to glaciers, are also found in deposits left by large meteors. New York University geologist Michael Rampino advanced the theory that catastrophic meteor collisions contributed to the geology we observe today, not slow ice ages. Again, billions or even millions of years are not needed.

In 1993, two reports filed by the Greenland Ice Core Project and the Greenland Ice Sheet Project, found no evidence supporting past climate instabilities beyond the last, *the only*, ice age (79).

Ice core rings are attributed to summer melt, and winter freeze. Science measured 263 feet of ice pack in only 48 years (from 1942 to 1990) in Greenland, which is up to 5½ feet per year. During these 48 years, the scientists did not find 48 ice rings, representing one for each year. The scientists discovered hundreds of rings, indicating hundreds of melts and freezes. It became obvious that the ice core rings represent not years, but melts, many of which can occur in a single year. The newer estimate for the Greenland Ice sheet is now 1,800 years of age, as opposed to the older estimate of over 4,000 years.

Dr. Donald W. Patten, Geographer, University of Washington, proposed a scientific answer to various unexplainable historic facts: 1) Mastodon, mammoths, rhinos, and other animals have been found *quick* frozen with buttercups and daises still in their mouths, 2) Solid ice formations exist, to this day, in volcanic tubes where water flow and temperature cannot create ice, and even further, they cannot support ice existing for thousands of years, much less tens of thousands of years, 3) The size and volume of the "ice age" cannot be explained by any scientific method. The ice is estimated by scientists to have been 15-20 million cubic miles of frozen water, and the ice was divided between the two _magnetic_ poles, north and south (not the two _geographic_ poles). The ice rose to heights of 17,000 feet, covering an area of 11,000 square miles. To form 17,000 feet of ice would require over one million inches of snow-fall. No scientific explanation by conventional science can explain how this happened, yet the evidence supports that somehow it did. If the ice were to have been spread evenly over the entire planet, it would make an ice layer about 400 feet thick. Ice, to this day, is still located 5,000 feet below sea level at the pole in an otherwise salty ocean basin. All this evidence, points to some catastrophic event, at the time of the mammoths, about 5,000 years ago. Science has determined that the mammoths suffered asphyxiation resulting from temperatures at or below -150 degrees. Autopsies performed upon these frozen animals show that they were all quick frozen in approximately five to fifteen minutes.

Either an Axial shift in the earth's rotation, or a Mantle shift of the earth's land masses would result in catastrophic disaster for all the earth. Brent Miller in 2016 has stated that the Axial shift would better fit the evidence of quick frozen mammoths and also numerous cities submerged under hundreds of feet of ocean water today—dating to a time thousands of years ago. The earth spins on a 23.5 degree shift today. If the earth used to spin closer to a 0 degree axis in pre-history, this would explain how cities now under water existed on dry land, and also explain how green forests and plant life have been discovered under the ice in the Antarctica, seemly quick frozen themselves. This shift would have caused the great flooding that geology records.

Reports in 2018 and 2019 by Michael J. Oard conclude that there was only one Ice age, and the ice dome geology of Keewatin and Queen Elizabeth Islands in Canada, as well as the islands and seas north of Norway are explainable only by this ice age after a flood.

Another possibly related problem for conventional science is trying to explain the formation of granite (which seems to only form in a cold state—not hot or molten). Science theorizes the state that the planet was in early in the planets formation was hot and molten, and granite could not form—yet it exists.

Dr. Patten theorizes that about 5,000 years ago (at the time of the freezing of the mammoths), the earth's orbit passed within 10,000 miles of some asteroid, comet, or possibly even an icy moon object, and further, this object would have been at least 250 to 280 miles in diameter (in order to contain enough water and ice). As our earth's orbit passed within 10,000 miles of this icy object, the object would break apart, and the resulting ice particles would have entered into earth's gravitational and magnetic fields. The

ice would drop mostly upon the two magnetic regions (ice particles can take on magnetic charges), causing a massive freeze in
these two polar (magnetic) regions, just as science records. Some
of the ice particles would fall in the warmer regions of the earth as
rain, and cause flooding. The massive ice formations at the poles
would then begin to melt, causing periods of flooding, and raising
of the sea levels, which scientific evidence supports. This type of
comet, asteroid, or icy moon capture, and breakup by earth, could
explain today's catastrophic geologic make-up, and unnatural scientific facts, which otherwise, cannot be explained by conventional
science today.

Another theory, regarding catastrophic events, points to an
area of study called earth-crust displacement (80). Some scientists,
including Albert Einstein, suggest that at certain periods in earth's
history, the entire earth's crust can slip or rotate. One can imagine
that this would cause massive geologic displacements and volcanic
activity, along with immediate worldwide extinctions. This displacement would create an ice cap where one never existed before.

On Mars, crustal displacement is theorized to cause the unique
signature pattern of impact craters. An article, by Peter Schultz, in
1985, in *Scientific American,* points to areas on Mars, outside the
polar regions, which have the same pattern caused by ice and meteorite impacts as the current polar region.

In his book, *Catastrophism and the Old Testament,* geographer
Dr. Donald Patten, along with physicist and orbital analyst Robert
Hatch, point out a cyclical pattern in earth's ancient history where
crustal displacement coincides with major recorded events. These
catastrophic events occur in 54-year cycles. These slippages or
displacements of the earth's crust, they suggest, were caused by
the planet Mars, in early epochs, crossing in very close proximity
to the orbit of the earth. These close encounters of Mars and earth
occurred up until the last recorded major event, in the year of 701
B.C. This last catastrophic encounter caused Mars to shift into its
current orbital pattern, which no longer crosses the earth's orbit.

It is interesting to note that around this period of 700 B.C. is
also when the 360-day calendar had to be changed to 365.25 days,
and the 30-day moon cycle was changed to 29.5 days. Prior to this

period, of 700 B.C., the 360-day calendar with a 30-day moon cycle was used by nations all over the world including Arabia, Assyria, Babylonia, China, Egypt, Greece, India, Japan, Mexico, Israel, Persia, Peru, and Rome. Some of these ancient cultures are known to have possessed knowledge of square roots and trigonometry. Therefore, their calendars should have been highly accurate. After 701 B.C., evidently earth's orbit increased one-seventieth to 365.25 days, and the moon's orbit decreased one-seventieth to 29.5 days (See the Globe Time Chart in the Appendix).

Dr. William Cooper (historian, England), notes that if Genesis were written during, or after, the captivity of the Israelites in Babylon (after 6th and 5th centuries B.C.), they would have used the Babylonian and Persian calendar calculations (month and days), which the Jewish people did use in all other daily functions. However, when the days and months are written of in Genesis, exact 30-day months are referenced (5 months of 150 days— Genesis 7:11-8:4). During, and after the Jewish people were in Babylon, they used the existing knowledge of days and months, which required 29 days and other adjustments, which they still use, even today. Genesis, however, is very specific as to 30 days, which agrees with the monthly patterns which would have been in existence before the massive break-up of the earth, due to the flood, and further earth-splitting, which science agrees occurred in the past as Pangaea (the one land mass), broke up into the continents we observe today.

The Mayan calendar uses 360-day years, but in the first century B.C. (2,100 years ago), they began adding five extra days they called the "ill omen days." The Inca calendar is the world's most accurate calendar with an accuracy of seven significant figures.

The oldest calendar in the world is Chinese, at 4,700 years, and it uses 360-day years. Going back in time 4,700 years, also points to a period that scientists using Paradigm B would call a period of great flooding, when civilizations began.

These close encounters by Mars would explain the unusual pattern of "magnetic reversals" which geologists have discovered recorded in the earth's rocks. Conventional science (paradigm A), theorize that the earth's core reverses every 10,000 to 50,000 years to recharge the magnetic field, which additionally causes the north and south poles to reverse, or flip, each time. However, Paradigm B scientists note that while actual evidence does show magnetic changes, in certain areas of the planet, there is no evidence of overall pole reversals, or a flip. Geologists, by calculating the number of these theoretical "reversals," have estimated the origin of these Earth-Mars encounters to have begun approximately 12,000 years ago. These events recurred every 54 years, causing catastrophic events to occur on earth, the severity of which depended upon how close the two planets came to each other. These "magnetic reversals" are not universal around the world, but occur randomly, as isolated events. The overall magnetic pattern around the whole world shows periods of strength and weakness, but not pole reversals. We are currently in a period of the weakest-ever magnetic measurements.

Reports in 2018 from Jake Hubert, PhD., establish that Earth's magnetic field is decaying too quickly for it to be even 100,000 years old. Additionally he reports that planets and moons are still very hot and still losing large amounts of energy. If the planets and moons were very old, they would already be cold.

Encounters between Earth and Mars could have caused the Earth's crust to have slipped hundreds, even thousands of miles. These slippages would, of course, cause major events such as flooding, earthquakes, and volcanic activity, all within a short time period, which is in opposition to the conventional theory of slow sedimentary build-up and slow plate tectonics.

Sudden crust movement could answer many questions which conventional theories of plate tectonics cannot. Problems, such as how formations all around the world, from the Grand Canyon, to the Himalayas, show evidence of sudden formation in their rock layers. These rock layers show evidence of bending and curving, as if they had been formed while still soft, as part of a one-time event. Conventional theories of slow plate tectonics and sedimentation cannot account for all these geologic patterns. It is interesting to note that all the mountain ranges in the world show evidence, at the very top of the mountains, that they were once part of the ocean floor. Not only are clams found at the top of these highest peaks, including Mt. Everest, the highest peak, but many of these clams are found in the closed position, which means they were buried while still alive, and could not open up. Furthermore, Bob Cornuke, in a 2007 *National Geographic Documentary*, reported that clams found at 14, 000 feet still had organic material in them. This material was still testable, and this material tested to less than 40,000 years—not millions.

Dr. John Morris, in an article titled, *"When did the mountains rise?"* has collected data from various investigators, along with a similar chart from Ollier and Pain in *"The Origin of Mountains,"* and they note that all mountains around the whole world seemed to have come into existence at the same basic time, all during the same period of earth activity. *Scientific American,* in September of 2005, in a special edition on Earth (pages 26-27), reports that geologists agree that the earth was covered with a worldwide flood with waters up to 800 feet higher than today's sea levels, and giant mountain ranges were formed in the aftermath of this global event. This flood, they say, also accounts for massive extinctions seen around the world at about the same time. Of course, these scientists say this occurred between 120 and 125 million years ago, whereas, the Bible states this occurred about five thousand years ago.

Remember, that science also states that the mountains will totally erode in 14 million years, yet they are still here. Furthermore, they appear sharp and hardly eroded at all—quite young in fact. Today, seventy percent of earth is covered with water. If the earth were flat (the mountains eroded and flattened), there is enough water to cover the planet, up to a depth of 7,500 feet—about a mile-and-a-half.

Whether one's paradigm is based on conventional theories of plate tectonics, or various evidences of crust displacement, it seems that evidence does show the great pyramids have remained consistently aligned along the east-west plane, over thousands of years, while other ancient structures, located further away (such as the first temple at Jerusalem), seem to have shifted several degrees. Large land masses such as India, Alaska, and Antarctica have shifted hundreds of miles. If the earth's crust did shift, it appears the location of the pyramids of Egypt may have been at the center of the shift (not rotating), as they point correctly to the N, S, E, and W, while areas around the pyramids shifted.

It is noted, in the book *Path of the Pole,* that not one of the ice caps which built up around the earth in previous so-called "ice ages," occurred at either one of the present poles. What conventional science views as Ice Age advancement to areas of Asia, Africa, and Australia, may actually be examples of former polar regions, which have been displaced to their present position.

To quote Albert Einstein (80), "*In a polar region there is continual deposition of ice, which is not symmetrically distributed about the pole. The earth's rotation acts on these unsymmetrically deposited masses, and produces centrifugal momentum that is transmitted to the rigid crust of the earth. The constantly increasing centrifugal momentum produced in this way will, when it has reached a certain point, produce a movement of the earth's crust over the rest of the earth's body....*"

Antarctica has forests frozen under ice over a mile thick, and each year, 293 cubic *miles* of new ice are added to the polar region (81). It is possible that at one time, Antarctica was in a temperate zone, and that the entire continent shifted to the pole, where it rests today. Even since 2012, during the theoretic "Global Warming" period where the western Antarctic ice is shrinking, the overall Antarctic ice volume continues to grow.

The reluctance of conventional science to accept recent catastrophic events in earth's history may be changing. Discoveries, showing that asteroid and meteor activity has occurred relatively recently in earth's history, are causing science to include catastrophic events in their calculations, thereby, changing theories.

Scientists, such as Victor Clube, of Oxford University, and David Raup, of the University of Chicago, point out that theories of uniform development of the planet are giving way to evidence, showing clearly, that catastrophic events have occurred recently in earth's history causing tremendous change. These catastrophic events not only can bring on geologic change and mass extinctions, they can also help explain oil and coal deposits, which theoretically took millions of years to develop through slow sedimentary deposits.

Oil and coal formation have been attributed, by conventional scientists, to processes involving long time periods, millions of years. Analysis of oil has provided data that a chemical found in crude oil, and blood, and also in plants, called porphyrin, breaks down very rapidly in the presence of oxygen or heat. Petroleum porphyrins have been identified in a sufficient number of sediments and crude oils, to establish a wide distribution of these geo-chemical fossils around the world (22). These high porphyrin levels are not possible without rapid burial, as is possible in flooding and catastrophic events, and *not* slow sedimentary buildup, which would expose the chemicals to oxygen. Additionally, research tests of DiNello and Chang, along with Fuhrhop and Smith, shows the formation of petroleum porphyrins can be produced, not in millions, or even thousands of years, but in a matter of hours (23). Thus, paradigm B, with a young earth age, is supported by oil studies, both from formation of a rapid burial.

Nobel prize medalist, Dr. Melvin Cook, has studied oil and gas well pressures and the permeability of the surrounding trap formation. He has concluded that oil and gas deposits have resulted from sudden, deep burial of organic material, a relatively short time ago (62). Cook notes that abnormally high pressures (up to 8,000 pounds per square inch), found relatively frequently in deep oil wells, points out that the oil has not been in the ground for a long period. Using the measured values of the permeability of the rock surrounding the oil well, it is possible to compute the time it will take for the oil to seep through the rocks to the surface and the infinity of the surrounding strata. Cook reported that the time required for a typical oil well to dissipate in this manner is on the order of as little as 4,000 years. These calculations are based upon the dynamics of fluid flow through porous media, an area of science that is considered to be well-proven and non-controversial.

Recently, E.F. Blick made similar calculations for deep gas geopressured reservoirs and found that the high gas pressures would dissipate in periods shorter than 10,000 years (63). Again, pointing to a young age for gas deposits.

In 2014, Tim Clarey PhD. published studies on reservoirs of hydrocarbons and oil processes which form rapidly—not requiring millions of years. Even secular scientists agree that non-biodegradable oils may be the result of recent recharge in the oil fields, and some depleted oil fields may partially refill over the next century. Oil can be produced from algae, from bugs, and even from e-coli working on wood chips and straw.

Thomas Gold, in a book, "*Deep Hot Biosphere*," notes that evidence supports oil, gas, and coal, as having origins from deep in the earth due to bacteria growth within the geologic layers, not just "fossil" sources from plant and animal deposits. Oil and gas wells are actually refilling as the result of the continual bacteria growth. Evidence would point to a young age for these deposits, because old wells are refilling so quickly today. Evidence of "life matter" in oil and coal includes mostly bacteria life forms from within the earth, and not much of this life matter is actually from surface life, such as the burial of the dinosaurs etc., which was the theory of conventional scientists. As of 2008, Russia is experiencing an explosion in oil deposit discoveries, and they are using this bacteria theory of oil, the abiotic origin of oil, and its special geologic requirements, to locate deposits, instead of traditional fossil fuel methods.

In New Zealand and Australia, sewage is being converted to oil in just 30 minutes, showing that long periods of millions of years are not necessary for the formation of our oil fields.

Coal is also shown to be a product of rapid burial, such as that of a flood, or other catastrophic events. Scientists using the parameters of paradigm A suggest that coal resulted from gradual sedimentary formations, involving millions of years. Evidence, however, supports paradigm B, rapid burial, and a young earth. It is very common to find marine fossils, including fish, mollusk and brachiopods, in coal, along with fossils of plants and animals not associated with marine swamps (24). Often, tree trunks are found extending through several strata of coal beds, sometimes upside down. The hollow trunks of these trees are commonly filled with rocks unlike the immediate surrounding rocks. Again, evidence supporting a rapid burial, such as a flood. These fossils, such as trees, which extend up through several layers, are called "polystrate fossils," and they are very common. National

Geographic published pictures from Tennessee, showing a fos-silized tree extending upward through several layers of coal, embedded shale, as well as several other thin layers of earth. The tree was preserved, meaning that all of those layers formed as a result of one single catastrophic event.

Studies have been done on boulders found in coal fields all over the world. P.H. Price determined many of the boulders are unlike any rock outcrops in the surrounding area of the coal fields (25). Experiments in the alteration of vegetable material show that coal resembling anthracite does not require millions of years to form, but can be produced rapidly by a short heating process (26). Coalification has also been observed in many underground mine fires, all of this further demonstrating rapid formation and a young earth.

Coal can be made out of grass in only hours by science today. Coal fields show texture, like rapid burial of chunks of vegetation, whereas, peat bogs with slow sediment build up show texture like coffee grounds. Obviously, our coal fields were the result of rapid burial, such as that which occurs in a major flood.

There is still further evidence of a young earth. This comes from the decaying magnetic field of the earth, which scientists, from both paradigms of thought, A and B, have verified. All agree the magnetic field deteriorates over a 10,000 year period. Unless there is some method to "recharge" the field strength, the magnetic field will drop to zero eventually. Scientists who conceptually need an earth billions of years old, have put forth a *theory* that sug-gests there is a dynamo below the earth's surface, which "reverses" polarity every 10,000-70,000 years or so, after the field of magne-tism falls. This theory has been severely challenged in recent years (27), and observations and measurements have given even more evidence of a young earth, supporting paradigm B. Magnetic pat-terns worldwide are stronger and weaker, not "reversals." So called polarity "reversals" are not universal. From the article in "Science" (in June 2003, Vol. 300, pages 2044-5), the conclusion concerning long term changes in Earth's magnetic field is that there are *no* strong theoretical arguments supported by any evidence to con-clude that magnetic field reversals, and related field strengths, are worldwide universal events. Localized events which cause "reversals" are such things as volcanic activity, asteroid impacts, and other such cataclysmic events in history, but they do not suggest a core reversal of the earth.

Measurements of archea-magnetic data from ancient pottery, bricks, etc., has shown a general overall rate of decay, even though there was a measured period of violent changes, up and down in magnetic strength, thousands of years ago (28), which are attributed to catastrophic events, such as great flooding, volcanic activity, and earthquakes, which have occurred in earth's history. Paleo-magnetic data confirm the existence of multiple order components, such as quadra-poles, and octa-poles, in the past, explainable by these catastrophic events. These fluctuations and "reversals" show up in measurements dating back about 4,500 years ago, and have diminished since the last smaller fluctuation, occurring about 1,500 years ago (29). Measurements accounting for maximum field strength, the fluctuations and oscillations since that catastrophic period in Earth's history, and the current measured decay, place a maximum age for the earth at 10,000 years. This is the upper limit (30).

Science and News, from a report by Thomas Sumner in 2016 point to a magnetic field that is stronger than previously thought. Still, Vernon Cupps PhD., in 2016, also noted that the strength of the field is continually decaying. The reduction in strength does match with a young earth model, where it would still have strength after several thousand years, but does not match with an old earth model, where the field should have disappeared long, long ago if the earth is billions of years old. Cupps further reported that Dr. Humphres' estimates of magnetic field strength reduction for other planets based upon young age has proven valid. Dr. Humphres predicted that Mercury's field strength should have been reduced between the Mariner 10 probe of 1974 and the Messanger spacecraft's readings in 2013 by 4% based upon an age for the Solar System of only 6,000 years—and this proved to be true!

Further evidence related to magnetic field strength, supporting a young age for the solar system, comes from the data collected by the *Voyager II* space probe, as it measured Uranus and Neptun when it passed by them in space. Both planets displayed a decaying magnetic field in agreement with Earth's, in age. Dr. Jason Lisle, Ph.D. in Astrophysics, at the University of Colorado studied the satellite data from the NASA program and concluded that the magnetic fields of all the planets are still too strong to be very old. The Voyager spacecraft also measured a planetary tilt of axis, which cannot be explained by the dynamo theory of conventional scientists, using paradigm A (31). This measured tilt supports observations and data used by scientists whose parameters are from paradigm B, and further supports a young age of the earth and the solar system.

A controversial theory put forth by Professor Gregory Ryskin, in "Chemical and Biological Engineering" (Northwestern University, Ill.), states that there is no real proof of any "core" of the earth being responsible for the earth's magnetism. He theorizes that earth's magnetism is actually linked to ocean movements, where the salt in winter allows it to conduct electricity. This, of course, would point to a young planet.

There is factual evidence of an earth less than 10,000 years old. There are only theories of older *ages*.

RADIOMETRIC DATING

Age of Rocks
See *Target Truth Ministries.com*
for News & Updates

Geologists are divided into two groups, with the paradigm A group (conventional), using various radioactive elements to attempt to prove old earth age, and the paradigm B scientists questioning these techniques, and instead, using other evidence to prove a young earth.

There are serious problems with a great variety of possible experimental errors and shaky assumptions, according to Nobel Prize medalist, Dr. Melvin Cook (62). In fact, many dates have had to be discarded because of too many variables. For example, in the *Journal of Geophysical Research* (Vol. 73, No. 14), it is reported that lava rocks formed in 1800 and 1801 in Hualalai, Hawaii, show an age of formation of 160 million to 3 billion years, by using the potassium-argon dating method. The report goes on to say that these dates do not prove valid, as the rocks are *known* to have been formed by volcanic action in 1800-1801. Another report, in *Science* (Vol. 162, pg. 265), shows potassium-argon dates of 12 to 21 million years for volcanic rocks *known* to be less than 200 years old.

The age for a rock is when it is formed, such as when it cools after a volcanic eruption. Mount St. Helens erupted in 1980, and its rocks date from 2.4 to 2.6 million years old, instead of 1980. Bear in mind that radiometric materials are not found in sedimentary rock so only volcanic rock can be used to date these flows.

The potassium-argon technique measures the rates of how potassium-40 decays to argon-40, a gas that can remain trapped within minerals when they form. This technique has also been used on the Grand Canyon. The Grand Canyon has been tested on both the Cardenas Basalt Layer, an agreed upon "older" layer, and the recent lava flows of the western sections. Results again failed, as the younger lava rock tested "older" (33). These same Grand Canyon layers have also been tested with the rubidium-strontium 86 method, which is based upon the theory that rubidium-strontium decays to strontium-87, with strontium-86 remaining constant, and from this, a ratio can be derived to measure age. Again, the younger rocks tested older than the old rocks. The only difference between the two methods of measurements was that the potassium-argon method gives *very* old age numbers, and rubidium-strontium gives *extremely* old age numbers.

There are obvious problems with both systems, due to assumptions about the original amount of these radio-materials in the rocks. This original amount must be known in order to make accurate measurements. However, no scientists were recording information in the beginning. Therefore, scientists using paradigm A (and conventional theories of old age), *assume* quantities to fit into the old age theories. Another problem with these various techniques is that it is known that many of the daughter elements can easily be leached in and out of the rock. Harold Slusher (64), points out that tests show up to 80 percent of potassium, in samples of meteorite, was removed by running water over it for four-and-a-quarter *hours* and this could move the age of rocks to tremendously high old age numbers. And further, concerning the daughter elements (if there any originally in the rock), the *assumption* is made that in the beginning of the earth, there were *no* daughter elements initially present. Sidney P. Clementson, a British consulting engineer, however, has found very large amounts of daughter elements present in very young volcanic rock (65).

Uranium-thorium is another method used, which is subject to all these same problems. Uranium-238 decays to lead-206 plus helium. The ratio of the two in rock, it is theorized, will compute the age. Henry Fall, in his book *Age of Rocks,* pointed out that useful ages cannot be determined due to: 1) Uranium being leachable by ground water, 2) Radon gas moving easily in and out of rock systems, and the products of uranium and lead include radon, radium, and lead-210, and 3) Shells, common to rock formations, are sources for both uranium and lead. Of course, fourth on the list would be the *assumption* by paradigm A scientists that *no* lead-206 existed in Earth's beginning. Clementson, a British engineer, recently made a study of 18 rock samples from 12 volcanoes, as published in the U.S.S.R., and 10 samples from Faial Azores, Tristan da Cuuha, and Mt. Vesuvius (65). In *all* cases, the calculated uranium-lead ages were millions and billions of years, but the rocks were *known* to be quite young.

Further evidence comes from Nobel Prize medalist, Dr. Melvin Cook (62), who points out that free neutron capture may completely invalidate the uranium-thorium method. His analysis of uranium ore, from Katanga and Canada, showed no lead-204, little or no thorium 232, but a significant amount of lead-208. Since the lead-208 could not have come from common lead contamination, nor from thorium decay, it must have come from lead-207, by neutron capture. This would mean that radio-genic isotopes of lead found anywhere, can be accounted for by this process, and have *no* relation to age.

There are indicators from various radiometric techniques, using uranium, which indicate ages of strata systems in thousands, not millions or billions of years (34). Dr. Robert Gentry, in the *Annual Review of Nuclear Science* (36), gives radiometric evidence that the basement rock of Earth was formed in a cool state, not a molten condition. His research involves the study of pleochroic halos (colored spheres), produced by the radioactive decay of polonium-218. He analyzed over 100,000 of these halos in granite rocks, which had been taken from considerable depths below the land surface, and in all parts of the world. This radioactive element was primordial, in the original granite, and because the halos can only be formed in the crystals of the granite, and because the polonium-218 half-life is *only 3 minutes,* the granite had to cool and crystallize suddenly. The polonium-218 would have been gone before *molten* granite could have cooled.

Halos, in other minerals, can be shown to give equally startling evidence of a young earth. To this day, no one knows how granite formed (see section on Ice). If you melt down granite, and allow it to cool, it does not form granite. Granite must form in a cool condition. Crystals in granite rock (Zircons), have uranium and thorium, which produce helium as they decay. The helium escapes very rapidly from the rock. But, experiments as of 2013, reported by Dr. John Morris, show that granite rock still has high levels of helium, meaning a young age for granite, as the helium has not yet escaped. This evidence shows that these rocks are only about 6,000 years old. If they were millions, much less billions of years old, the helium would have totally escaped.

Additionally, Dr. Aardsma is experimenting on the theory, as mentioned earlier, that if the speed of light is indeed decaying, then also the decay rates of radioisotopes would have been greater in the past, further matching the observations with actual measurements of young earth age.

It was noted in December 1991, in *Newsweek,* that physicist Anthony Turkevich and two colleagues reported in the *Journal of Physical Review Letters,* that decay rates could be up to *100 times* faster than previously thought, which, of course, would mean a young age for everything from rocks to fossil bones. This error in measuring is attributed to the recent discovery of neutrinos, and how their mass affects decay rates and measurement techniques (35). Cosmic radiation and neutrino effect have, at the very least, thrown all radiometric methods into serious doubt.

Larry Vardiman Ph.D., and Professor Claus Rolfs of Ruhr University in Germany, report that decay rates could be increased 100 to 800 times faster as temperatures are reduced, thus, increasing the number of alpha and beta particles being ejected from the nucleus. Long time periods are not needed (see section on Ice).

Alternate dating methods, such as helium measurement, show much younger ages for the earth and life. Estimating by the rate of addition of helium to the atmosphere from radioactive decay, the age of the earth proves to be about 10,000 years old, even calculating for helium escape (37).

Dr. Jim Mason, Nuclear Physicist, states that radio-metric dating doesn't actually measure age at all. Rather, it measures the ratio of the radioactive "parent" element to the stable "daughter" element in a sample found today. The age must be inferred by using these measurements in a calculation, and this relies on several unverifiable assumptions...such as *"that there was no daughter element present when the rock was formed—i.e. the daughter element is entirely due to decay of the parent in the sample; that no amount of either parent or daughter has leached into or out of the rock since its formation; and that decay rate has not changed over time. If any of these assumptions are incorrect, it can dramatically change the calculation of age."*

Jim Mason, Nuclear Physicist, also reports that Carbon 14 (C-14), data is widely used to measure age of both rocks and life (see next section), as it is easily absorbed by plants and life along with Carbon 12. C-14 totally decays in 90,000 years, and yet it is found in coal fields all over the world which are theorized to be 30 to 400 million years old. Even diamonds, which are theorized to be 1 to 3 billion years old still possess levels of C-14 just like the coal beads.

So, how are the rock layers really dated? Not by radio-metric dating as many assume. Radio-metric dating is used to corroborate the assumed age *after* an age has already been assigned by another method. The rock layers are originally dated by the "index" fossils found in them. Radio-metric dating gives such a wide range of ages that it can only be use *after* the general age has been already identified. Index fossils are fossils not observed very often in other layers of rock. 99% of fossils are found commonly in many rock layers, whereas there are a few rare fossils that are *mostly* confined to a single rock layer (although they can be observed in layers earlier and later in age as well). So, how are the fossils dated? The truth is that it is evolutionary *theory* which is used to date these fossils, not the rocks they are found in.

There is plenty of evidence that the earth is less than 10,000 years old. The problem for conventional scientists, using paradigm A of old age, is that they can't provide any solid evidence of really "old" age—only theories.

CARBON—14 DATING

Age of Fossils
See *Target Truth Ministries.com*
for <u>News & Updates</u>

The Carbon-14 dating technique is subject to the same restrictions and variables as other radiometric methods. Carbon-14 testing has shown its half-life varies from five to ten percent, depending upon its environment. The neutron in the environment of the nucleus is a stable particle, but as a free particle, the neutron has a half-life of only *eight minutes* (38). This is compared to the normal half-life in the range of 5,200-5,700 years.

Carbon-14 is formed in the upper atmosphere by nitrogen being converted by cosmic radiation to C-14. Plants and animals utilize this C-14, as well as ordinary C-12, as they are absorbed with equal ease by tissues and cells. C-14 decays to nitrogen. When a plant or animal dies, it no longer utilizes carbon, and the trapped C-14 in the tissue begins to decay. By measuring the ratio of C-12 to C-14, an age can be assigned.

When this process was first developed and used, certain *assumptions* were made. One assumption was that the ratio of C-14 to C-12 in our atmosphere today has always been constant. Measurements, however, made by the U.S. space program recently, have found that the upper atmosphere has much more C-14 than estimated, which invalidated all previous dating.

It seems that scientists, *assuming* that the earth is billions of years old, also assumed that the ratio of C-12 to C-14 had reached equilibrium long ago. Calculations show that the equilibrium of C-12 to C-14 would take 30,000 years. When the U.S. space program found higher levels of C-14 at high altitude, it was proof that equilibrium had not yet been reached and, in fact, that thousands of years ago, there was even less C-14 than today. Again, this provides proof of a young age for the earth.

Also, as mentioned earlier, the earth shows evidence of a greater magnetic field in the past, which would have reduced the quantity of C-14 in the atmosphere, thus, making measured dates appear very "old," when they were actually very young. If a plant absorbs less C-14, then it appears old to scientists. The earth has lost six percent of its magnetic field strength in the last 150 years, and currently the field strength is at its lowest ever recorded.

Additionally, as mentioned earlier, if as studies show, the speed of light and atomic constants are slowing down, then the decay rates of C-14 and other radioisotopes would change, proving again, a young age for everything measured.

The best evidence is from actual measurements of plant and animal matter and their relationship to geology. If a specimen is older than 50,000 years, it is *undatable* by C-14 methods, because *all* usable, or reliable C-14 material would have decayed away already. However, in fact, thousands of samples from strata, which *geologically* are supposed to be undatable, have been dated, using C-14. These strata samples cannot possibly be older than 50,000 years, despite theories by scientists using paradigm A, suggesting millions of years, because C-14 is still present.

As of 2003, scientists have been able to improve the testing and dating techniques of C-14 with ultra-sensitive instruments. Science is now able to extend their measurements up to 90,000 years—well beyond the lifetime of 50,000 years for C-14. But, science was surprised to discover that *all* specimens have measurable amounts of C-14 with these newer techniques. This means that *no* specimens can possibly be older than 90,000 years, much less millions and billions of years, as suggested by theories of evolution. These tests have been confirmed again in 2018.

Professor Robert Whitelaw, of Virginia Polytechnic, in a paper titled *Time, Life, and History in the Light of 15,000 Radiocarbon*

Dates, concluded that none were over seven thousand years old. A statistical analysis, by Professor Whitelaw, of the 15,000 specimens, showed a worldwide disappearance of man and animals for a long period, about 5,000 years ago. This would appear to be the result of a worldwide catastrophe. These specimens included wide varieties of material, including Neanderthal man bones, saber-tooth tigers, mammoths, coal, natural gas, crude oil, etc.

Specimens that Whitelaw studied included samples in strata, identified as being Pleistocene, Pliocene, and even Eocene, which are theorized by conventional scientists using paradigm A, as being up to fifty million years old. Also, specimens from deep ocean deposits and cores from 40 feet below ocean beds, which contain the detritus of the most primitive forms of life, have been dated by Professor Whitelaw. None of these "old" specimens, theorized to be millions of years old, can possibly be more than thousands of years old.

In fact, modern man and animals, along with extinct flora and fauna, all appear equally ancient and all appear suddenly in the fossil record, even in the same layers of rock, fully developed, with not one "link" having ever been found between species. (see the *Fossil* section)

Thousands of "dates" are listed in the *Journals of Radiocarbon and Science* of samples of strata, which "geologically" are supposed to be" *undatable"* by C-14. Additionally, coal from Russia and from the Pennsylvania Strata, supposedly 300 million years old, have been re-dated to 1680 years (39). A *freshly* killed seal was dated by C-14 to have died 1,300 years ago (41). *Living* mollusk shells were dated as being up to 2,300 years old (42). *Living* snail shells showed they had died 27,000 years ago, again, using scientific methods preferred by scientists using paradigm A, with flawed C-14 ratios.

Tree ring data is used today to correct for readings of C-14. There is supposedly an error of between -100 and -150 years, from about 1,000 A.D. to 50 B.C., and +200 to +800 years, from 500 B.C. to 5000 B.C., for C-14 data. For example, if a C-14 date shows 2,500 B.C., then the corrected date, correlated to tree ring data, would be +500 more years, or 3,000 B.C. The tree ring data assumes only one growth ring period of 45 days per year. Of course, trees have been known to have several growth periods of 45 days or more in a single year, so it turns out that C-14 readings (which science agrees are faulty), are being corrected by tree ring data (which also is known to be faulty). It has been found that all trees, even slow growing ones, respond dynamically to tiny environmental changes, even hourly changes in growing conditions. Unusual storms with abundant rainfall, interspersed with dry periods, can produce multiple rings, essentially one per major storm.

There are 27 separate layers of trees and sediment in Yellowstone Park, and evolutionists have for years suggested that each layer represents thousands of years, and therefore, if you multiply 27 by several thousand years each, you end up with evidence of evolution and millions of years. However, as Mount St. Helens has shown, it is very possible for a great flooding event to lay down several layers of trees, each in a separate layer of sediment. Studies done recently on the trees in Yellowstone Park, have shown that these 27 layers of trees all have *matching* tree rings, indicating they were once all part of a common forest which was destroyed in a great flood. I wonder which flood that was.

The difficulties with the radio-carbon and other radiometric dating methods are undeniably deep and serious. It should be no surprise that fully half of all the dates are rejected, even by conventional scientists using paradigm A methods. The wonder is that the remaining half are accepted. Once again, there is proof of life being no more than 10,000 to 15,000 years old, and only theories of its extremely old age.

FOSSILS, AGE, & EVOLUTION

See *Target Truth Ministries.com*
for News & Updates

O f all the areas of science relating to age, the fossil evidence is the most overwhelming. Scientists using paradigm A, need a long time frame in order to "naturally" (in theory anyway), give time for *macro* evolution to occur. Macro evolution requires that large amounts of *new* information be added to the DNA of a species, so that it can change into a different species – a new life form. Scientists disagree on whether complex DNA changes can occur without killing the species, as *all* studies show most mutations actually kill the next generation.

All science agrees that *micro* evolution, within species, does occur. This type of evolution occurs because the species selects information *already available* within its DNA. This micro evolution does not result in a different species, only changes within the species.

Scientists who believe in macro evolution (of one species changing into a different species), propose theories of a very old earth age, and also a very old age for fossils. Large periods of time are needed to support their supposed idea of species being able to change into different life forms. Additionally, in order for long time age theories and evolution to work, these fossils must appear in separate *ages*, or strata of rock. As mentioned earlier, these strata are theorized by some scientists to represent long ages of sedimentary buildup. Thus, dinosaurs are theorized to be from one age, and humans from another age. Of course, science has already proven (as shown in previous sections here), that the geologic columns of strata do not represent ages at all, but catastrophic events.

In fact, the actual fossil record in rock shows a young earth, catastrophic flooding, volcanic activity, even asteroid and meteor impacts. Animal and plant species suddenly appear fully developed in the fossil record, even in the same layer of rock, and there has never been any link found between species. *None* of the intermediate fossils that would be expected on the basis of the evolution model have ever been found between single-celled organisms and invertebrates, between invertebrates and vertebrates, between fish and amphibians, between amphibians and reptiles, between reptiles and birds or mammals, or between so-called lower mammals and primates (45).

Charles Darwin wrote in his book, *Origin of Species,* that there was no fossil evidence of evolution, but he was sure that the missing links would soon be found. None ever have. The fossil record shows numerous creatures, supposedly existing millions of years before even the dinosaurs, which are identical with creatures in existence today. These include snakes, birds, turtles, mammals, lizards, crocodiles, insects, sharks, and octopus.

The theories of Paradigm A scientists, that out of the early "soup," a single cell eventually formed, which then evolved, fails to recognize that a very simple basic cell is actually more complex that the space shuttle.

Science has theorized that in the early planet (three billion years ago), that there must have been *no* oxygen, because oxygen would cause oxidation, which would kill any early life forms.

Scientists such as Dr. Morris (73), however, have discovered in ancient amber, air bubbles which indicate there was actually more oxygen in the past, than there is now. In a study in 2007, Alexander Kaiser, physiologist at Midwestern University, has determined that ancient bugs were able to grow to larger sizes because there were indeed higher levels of oxygen in the past.

Medicine today, shows that by increasing the oxygen for patients, they heal faster. Hyperbaric chambers are used to speed up healing by allowing the patient to recover with increased oxygen levels. While some would question how people could have lived so long in the past (as stated in the Bible), and what caused the dinosaurs and plants to grow so large in the past, others have pointed out that if the oxygen levels were fifty-nine percent higher in the past, then a water canopy could have filtered out all the harmful radiation, allowing for all these things. The dinosaurs would have been needed to mow all the grass, which would have been growing so fast and abundant.

The dinosaurs have always been a source of "old age" theories, because scientists using paradigm A, *assumed* the creatures lived and died before humans ever "evolved." However, these are just *theories,* and as we have already discovered, verifiable dating methods used on rocks, and fossils, give us a date of about 7,000 years ago. Supposed ages in the layers of rock, suggesting billions of years, are only theories, which evidence does not support.

But, one may ask, if these giant creatures were around when humans were, why don't we find fossil evidence of them together, and why are there no references to giant beasts in history? The answer is that we *do* have fossil evidence, and there are written references to these beasts in history. The word "dinosaur" didn't appear as a word until the late 1800's, and therefore, the recording of these creatures would use different terms—even the Bible uses words such as monster, dragon, beast, behemoth, leviathan, etc.

Naturally, one would expect to find fossil evidence, as these would be preserved in rock. However, if only a small population of these now-extinct species survived the catastrophic events thousands of years ago, of flooding and asteroid collisions, before written history, there would not be too many historically recent encounters to record, either in rock or on paper, but there are some.

In 1983, geologist Donald Patton reported on fossil evidence of dinosaur tracks and human footprints together, in Russia, Australia, and the United States. One fossil actually had the human print inside the dinosaur print. Dr. Carl Baugh, paleoanthropologist, reported on fossils in one particular area of Glenrose, Texas. There, they found 203 dinosaurs prints, 57 human prints, bones from atracanthrasaurs, a verified human finger bone, and an ancient hammer tool (70).

Dinosaur footprints are found in several layers, suggesting not thousands of years between layers, but that this dinosaur was trying to escape a flood, and climbed several layers to do so. Trilobites, theorized to be 600 million years old (which is ten times older than the dinosaurs), have been found squashed under a human footprint, according to Kent Hovind.

The Paluxy River site in Glen Rose Texas has caused many to pause, due to fossilized dinosaur tracks which appear with human tracks. There have been many attempts to prove that these human footprints are actually human. The dinosaur tracks have been accepted by scientists, due to the rock area which correlates to the supposed old age of the dinosaurs, but few scientists will pronounce the other tracks as "human." However, more and more sites are being exposed with "human" tracks which appear in dinosaur era rock, or even with dinosaur tracks, and even other ancient life forms such as trilobites, which actually *predate* the dinosaurs.

Aaron Judkins from the Texas Institute of Omniology reports in *"Evolution and Human fossil Footprints"* of several sites—also from the Paluxy riverbed area, at Taylor trail site, and at the Upper Taylor Platform, at Mcfall Trail site—in Russian Turkmenistan, at the Koughitang-Tau dinosaur site—in Stinnett, Texas, at the Coffee track site—in Dinosaur Valley State Park, Texas, at the Delk track site—in Moenkopi Wash, Arizona—in Robledos mountains New Mexico, at Zapata track site—and in Antelope springs, Utah, at the Meister track site, where trilobites are commonly found. The human footprints found in these various sites have been found to have all the characteristics of "human" tracks, but because of their placement amongst dinosaurs and trilobites, they are dismissed as "unknown."

Many cultures throughout history have made reference to beasts, giants, or dragons. Such references appear in China, Japan, Australia, South America, India, Europe, England, and even in the Americas (71). We find that a Sumerian story, dating back to 3,000 B.C., tells of its hero encountering a huge, vicious dragon. When Alexander the Great marched into India over 2,000 years ago, they found the Indians worshiped huge reptiles that they kept in caves. Ancient American Indian drawings are done in the likeness of known fossil dinosaurs. From the Ta Prohm monastery in Cambodia dedicated in 1186, there is a Stegosaur carving on a column. Burial stones from Ica Peru, show dinosaurs and humans together. The tomb of Bishop Bell in England who died in 1496, shows a picture of a Sauropod dinosaur. China has a long history of dragon stories, and China, itself, is host to one of the largest dinosaur finds in the world. England has its story of St. George, who slew a dragon. In the tenth century, an Irishman wrote of his encounter with what appears to have been a stegosaurus. In the 1500's, a European scientific book, *Historia Animalium,* listed several animals (which to us are dinosaurs), as *still alive.* A well-known naturalist of the time, Ulysses Aldrovandus, recorded an encounter between a peasant, named Baptista, and a dragon, whose description fits that of the dinosaur, Tanystropheus. This encounter was dated May 13, 1572, near Bologna, in Italy. In 1980, on February 6, *The Melbourne Sun,* reported that more than forty people claimed to have seen plesiosaurs off the Victorian Coast of Australia, over recent years. In *Science Digest,* June 1981, and also in 1983, in *Science Frontiers, No. 33,* explorers and natives in Africa have reported sightings of dinosaur-like creatures.

Dr. Carl Werner, in his book "Living Fossils," reports on how researchers have found many modern bird remains along with dinosaurs—yet museums do not display the bird fossils—only the dinosaurs. Evolutionary "theory" states that birds evolved *from* dinosaurs (meaning *no* bird fossils should exist along with dinosaurs). Dr. Werner visited 60 natural history museums, ten dinosaur dig sites in seven different countries, and of the 60 museums he visited, not one single fossil of the modern birds which had been found in dinosaur rock layers was displayed. Ironically, according to Dr. Bill Clemens (an evolutionary paleontologist), the only reason the bird fossils came to light, is because there was a science project to discover evidence to disprove that an asteroid impact caused the extinction of dinosaurs, (a study to see if modern animals existed prior to the impact—not just after). Dinosaur hunters look for dinosaur fossils, and anything else discovered is of no interest—there is no money or fame to be made by finding a modern parrot along with a dinosaur, supposedly 70 million years old.

The point of these references is that it is entirely possible for a small population of many species of currently extinct plants and animals to have survived those catastrophic events of 5,000 years ago, as measured by Professor Robert Whitelaw, of Virginia Polytechnic, in his paper titled, *Time, Life, and History in the Light of 15,000 Radio-carbon Dates*. Several species have become extinct, due to catastrophic events and climate changes; however, there is no proof that evolution was ever involved. In fact, all species appear suddenly, together in the fossil record, with *no* missing links having ever been found. Some have become extinct, and the rest are still living.

In their book, *Forbidden Archeology,* in 1996 (85), Michael Cremo and Richard Thompson list pages of human fossils and artifacts found in rock strata, dated by the conventional means of paradigm A, to be millions, even billions of years old. All this evidence of human beings, living supposedly before the age of the dinosaurs, suggests either evolution is totally false, or a massive catastrophic event took place. A catastrophic event would account for the geologic strata being the way it is, not billions of years of sedimentation. Either way, the conventional view of science cannot be defended, and new theories are needed.

Acts and Facts magazine, June 2008, published actual pictures of various dinosaurs cut into rock (or depicted on drawings, etc.), by ancient cultures in Cambodia, Peru, Mexico, and North America. These all pre-date the "discovery" of dinosaurs in the 1800's. Obviously, humans and dinosaurs did co-exist as these pictures of what we, today, call dinosaurs are clearly pictured by early humans in these drawings and carvings.

The Associated Press released a news story, in December 1994, reporting that scientists discovered, in Australia, living trees that were thought to be "extinct" trees that were *believed* to have disappeared between the Jurassic and Cretaceous "ages" theorized to be 150 million years ago. In 2007, in New Zealand, similar finds were made. Obviously, these trees only went undiscovered for a few thousand years.

Additionally, Scott Woodward, a microbiologist at Brigham Young University, who is best known for identifying the genetic markers that led to the recent discovery of the defective gene causing cystic fibrosis, and also for his work with the Egyptian government in using DNA to untangle the family relationships of ancient dynasties, has shown that evolutionists are wrong in their theories of birds and reptiles evolving from dinosaurs. Dr. Woodward's studies of dinosaur DNA shows *no* relationship to birds or reptiles. The dinosaurs were their own group and they died. No long ages for evolution to occur are necessary.

It is very interesting that dinosaur bones, which supposedly died millions of years ago, turning into stone, are now able to give scientists soft tissue and blood, so as to extract DNA to study. In 2005, Mary Schweitzer of North Carolina State University, along with Bob Harmon, fossil preparer of the Museum of the Rockies, announced that soft tissue taken from dinosaurs, which has not fully fossilized, may be able to provide DNA data. In 2006, Philip Currie, curator of dinosaurs at the Royal Tyrrell Museum of Paleontology, and Eva Koppelhus, researcher, noted that *most* fossil dinosaur bones still contain the *original bone* (*not* actually fossilized, indicating recent burial). It was reported in 2015-2016 in *Science News*, that a 48 million year old horse had soft tissue within it of its uterus and placenta, and that "*the reproductive tract looks much like that found in horses today.*" Frank Sherwin M.A., reported in 2015, that in Canada plant tissue 53 million years old has been found with "*exquisitely preserved unfossilized wood and leaf.*" Also, protein had been discovered in dinosaur eggs from the early Jurassic. *Lifescience Magazine* reported in 2015 that fungus was found preserved in 2.7 million year old sediment—"*We've found diatoms and the nucleic acid (DNA) preserved in sediment for millions of years.*"

A *Smithsonian* magazine article by Clayton Phipps titled "Dinosaur Cowboy" reported how scientists for many years have reported discoveries of dinosaur "fossils" which are actually not truly "fossils." Scientists have reported that many dinosaur discoveries are actually of bone and tissue...even soft tissue which may hold DNA, and not actually fossilized bone (bone is only a fossil if it has been replaced by minerals to form a rock record of the original bone). "*There's an entire skin envelope around the dinosaurs. They're basically mummies. There could be soft tissue inside.*" Currently, these dinosaur discoveries are being housed in a storage facility at an undisclosed location in New York per the *Smithsonian* article. In 2017, it was reported that Dr. Adrian Lister, a British paleobiologist, stated how difficult it is to study DNA fragments from the Ice Age, convincing him that DNA cannot possibly last for millions of years.

Science News, in 2012, reported on human fossils supposedly 95,000 years old, still being testable for DNA. In 2016, *Science News* reported "exceptionally well preserved soft tissue which are the remains of a ventral nerve cord 520 million years old. Brian Thomas M.S., in 2016 reported on Duck Billed dinosaur soft tissue 80 million years old revealed ten different proteins with sequences of amino acids intact, even though science reports all protein structures cannot last beyond one million years. Scientists are debating this problem of testable DNA from fossils over 10,000 years old. Scientists Woodward, Weyand, and Bunnell, in an article in *Science* titled "*DNA Sequence from Cretaceous Period Bone Fragments*" have verified that the half-life of DNA has been determined to be 521 years (meaning that half of the testable DNA is untestable after 521 years—it deteriorates to a point where the chemical sequences become too short for modern science to sequence). Every 521 years, half of the remaining DNA is destroyed, making it impossible for DNA to be testable beyond the outer limit of 10,000 years. The DNA *sequences* cannot survive beyond 10,000 years, and absolutely *all* DNA chemical bonds are totally destroyed in 6.8 million years according to an article in *Popular Science* in 2013, reporting on test results from scientists in the "Proceedings of the Royal Society B."

Still, *Science News*, in 2012, along with *Nature*, reported that dinosaur discoveries in northeast China, dated to be 125 million years old, contain "*well preserved ancient dinosaurs, along with their soft tissues.*" Acts & Facts reported that soft tissue is being studied by scientists on Mosasaur fossils from 80 million years ago, and these tissues include eye retina, skin, and hemoglobin.

Dr. Adrian Lister, Paleobiologist, stated in studies in 2017, that DNA cannot survive in very old bones. Depending upon burial conditions, DNA cannot survive beyond 50,000 years…perhaps up to 1 million maximum. Therefore, he concludes, dinosaurs cannot be 50 to 125 million years old. Yet, in 2016, some scientists were still reporting on soft tissue and blood vessels from dinosaurs revealing DNA samples.

Further studies by George Poinar, Professor of Entomology at the University of California, and Raul Cano, Molecular Biologist of California Polytechnic State University, on DNA extracted from bees in amber, tested to be 20-40 million years old, by conventional scientists using parameters of paradigm A, have shown the "older" DNA to be the *same* as DNA found in modern bees *today*. Again, there is no evidence of evolution, or millions of years.

Brian Thomas M.S., in 2014 reported on finds in Burma/Myanmar where parts of birds, reptiles, fish, clams, plants, and mammals, were trapped and preserved in amber resin in strata near or below dinosaur fossils (by coal deposits assigned ages of 100 million years), and these various life forms look just like today's versions.

Even Charles Darwin recognized this problem, as he states in his book, *Origin of Species*: "*Long before the reader has arrived at this part of my work, a crowd of difficulties will have occurred to him. Some of them are so serious that to this day I can hardly reflect on them without being in some degree staggered. Why, if species have descended from other species by fine graduations, do we not see everywhere innumerable transitional forms? Why then is not every geological formation and every stratum full of such inter-mediate links? Geology assuredly does not reveal any such finely graduated organic chain, and this, perhaps, is the most obvious and serious objection which can be urged against the theory.*"

In the foreword of the centennial edition of Darwin's *Origin of Species*, published as part of *Everyman's Library Series*, Dr. W.R. Thompson writes: "*As we know, there is great divergence of opinion among biologists, not only about the causes of evolution, but even the actual process. This divergence exists because the evidence is unsatisfactory and does not permit any certain conclusion. It is therefore right and proper to draw the attention of the non-scientific public to the disagreements about evolution. But some recent remarks of evolutionists show that they think this unreasonable. This situation, where men rally to the defense of a doctrine they are unable to defend scientifically, much less demonstrate with scientific rigor, attempting to maintain its credit with the public by the suppression of criticism and the elimination of difficulties, is abnormal and undesirable in science."*

A physiologist with the U.S. Atomic Energy Commission, Dr. T.N. Tahmisian, says: *"Scientists who go about teaching that evolution is a fact are great con men, and the story they are telling may be the greatest hoax ever. In explaining evolution, we do not have one iota of fact."*

Our school textbooks often reference such things as "horse evolution," and "human embryo evolution," which are known to have been fabricated. These false evolutionary pictures are still in the textbooks supposedly because of lack of funding to replace them, according to educators.

Archeoptrics, a perching bird, which is theorized as a transitional link between dinosaurs and birds, was discounted as a link in 1986 by scientists, but is still referred to by school textbooks, and also still in science articles in periodicals.

Herbert Nilssen, Director of Botany Institute, Lund University, states: *"It is not even possible to make a caricature of evolution out of paleo-biological facts. The fossil material is now so complete that the lack of transitional series cannot be explained as due to the scarcity of the material. The deficiencies are real, they will never be filled. The idea of an evolution rests on pure belief."*

Professor John Koltz (66) wrote: *"In what is known as the Cambrian rock strata period, there is literally a sudden outburst of living things of great variety. Very few of the groups which we know today were not in existence at the time of this Cambrian rock."*

One of the problems of the Cambrian outburst is the sudden appearance of all these forms. All the animal phyla are represented already in the Cambrian strata. Two independent teams of paleontologists under D. G. Shu, and also Chen, Huang, and Li, reported in *Nature* science magazine in 1999, that all phyla have now been identified in the Cambrian layer, meaning that all life forms appear suddenly, at the same time, all phyla together at once. Evolutionists, in 2007, recognized that *trilobites* show their greatest variability in the beginning of the fossil record, in the Cambrian layer. Since that time, species have shown degeneration, and in more recent times, there are less varieties within species—just the opposite of what one would expect if evolutionary processes were creating new DNA information, and new life forms.

Tim Clarey PhD., in 2014, reported on how the Cambrian layer (the oldest layer), seems to preserve a record of a flood, and not eons of burials. Even Trilobites (creatures with compound eyes), the *theorized* oldest of creatures, are preserved in rolled up positions indicating they were buried while still alive. No transitional life forms are found. All life suddenly appears and is buried in the Cambrian. Within the Cambrian are found life forms with jointed legs and appendages, muscle systems, exoskeletons with a molting process of growth, antennae and nervous systems, respiratory organs and blood circulation systems, complex mouth parts, and jellyfish with triggered harpoon stinging cells. No transitions exist. Some life forms have gone extinct, while others still exist today.

World-renowned paleontologist George Gaylord Simpson (67) has stated: *"Fossils are abundant only from the Cambrian onward. Darwin was aware of this problem. Fossils would provide the only direct evidence of the earliest living things, (missing links), but none have been found."*

The hope of establishing a missing link between man and ape was dealt a serious blow when anthropologist, Richard Leakey, published evidence that Australopithecines were long-armed, short-legged, knuckle-walkers similar to extinct African apes (68), and in all probability, were just an extinct ape species. Even more shattering, was Leakey's discovery in 1972. He found bones which were similar to those of *modern* man, but were dated much *older* than Australopithecus and Peking Man (50, 69). Again, no missing links. Humans and apes appear simultaneously.

Archeology, Jan/Feb. 2008, reported that at Lake Ileret in Kenya, bones from modern man have been found together with bones of "homo habillis," supposedly millions of years old – oops.

It is interesting that the image of "ancient man" is of them living in caves. Actually, all fossils found in caves have been shown to be fully human. And, even today, people still live in caves, and still make stone tools. All these so-called fossils of theorized "human links" are *not* found in caves.

In their book, *Forbidden Archeology,* in 1996 (85), Michael Cremo and Richard Thompson commented on these finds by Richard Leakey, as well as many others, and they concluded: *"Given the total body of available paleo-anthropological evidence, we can only conclude that something must be seriously wrong with our current scientific picture of human evolution."*

The fossil record actually documents the *separate* origin of primates and all other forms (46). There are *no* fossil traces of a transformation from an ape-like creature to humans (47). The fossils of Neanderthal man are now classified as a human species, with no link to apes (48), and this was confirmed in *Science* in 2010, and confirmed again in 2019 by Dr. Robert Carter. Ramapithecus was once considered to be partly manlike, but is now known to be fully ape (49). Piltdown man and Nebraska man, once thought to be missing links, have been proven false (51). Recent detailed evidence has caused theories on the evolution of the horse to be discarded, as the fossil record disproves any possibility of evolution (52).

In an effort to support evolutionary theories and fit the famous "Lucy" bones into human ancestry, and date them to four million years ago, science is using other related bone finds as supporting evidence. The recent discoveries of the Ananemsis series of bones are being used for this purpose. These fragments total 21 pieces, and are from two separate finds, 100 miles apart from each other. One arm bone from the first find, thirty years ago, was deemed human and would not fit with the other fragments, which were ape-like. This arm bone was shelved by scientists, because they couldn't explain how a fully human bone was mixed in with evolving links, assumed to be four million years old.

This problem surfaced again recently, with the new discovery of a second set of fragments found in this same Kanapoi area of Africa. In this find, a shin bone (also very much human), was discovered with a group of supposedly four million year-old ape-like bones. It should be noted that all these bones and fossils are dated by the "geology" of the area, so theories and assumptions abound. Science cannot explain why ape-like, theoretically transitional bones, four million years old, are found with fully human bones just like ours. Of course, only the supposedly four million year bones were made public.

Scientific American, in 2009, reported that the *"Tree of Life"* (the familiar tree of evolution), has been completely wrong all these years and must now be replaced with a radically new model. The article focused on the recent discovery of the fossil "Ardi," which supposedly gives a new picture of how evolution led to humans. This is one more example of science revising their hypothesis to accommodate new finds, but never recognizing that their basic assumptions of age are flawed. Science has since determined that the fossils of Ardi were so poor (bones seriously crushed, the feet having a huge opposable toe, and no arch like human feet, etc.), that it is now thought to be just another example of an extinct primate.

William Hoesch, MS, geologist, in an article titled: *"How Coherent is the Human Evolution Story?"* notes that leading anthropologists find the differences between various human fossil categories to be so small that they have wondered "in print" if Homo Sapiens and Homo Erectus are one and the same. They also noted that many so-called "old traits" are actually found in some current families of humans, such as Eskimos. They also noted that supposedly "older" human forms are found also in "later" rock strata, and supposedly "later" forms are found in "older" rock strata. Furthermore, these anomalies are not rare, but numerous.

Science has argued about whether Neanderthal DNA is within the range of modern human or not. Some scientists are theorizing that Neanderthal may have interbred, while other scientists say there was never any relationship between them and other humans. This is discussed by Matthais Krings in *"Cell #9,"* and it appears that this is a case of *micro*-evolution, where there are divergent species within the humankind, but not *macro*-evolution where humans evolve from primates.

In 2016, scientists reported in *Science News* that Human DNA has now been discovered in Neanderthal bones. Jeffery Tomkins

PhD., reports that sequences of Neanderthal and Denisovans actually match Human sequences 99.7% to 100%.

Christoph Zollikofer, Anthropologist, has reported on a skull claimed to be 1.8 million years old, that shows that many old skulls actually are quite similar to modern man, and that all the various supposedly different species were actually all just one species—Homo erectus.

Today, evidence points towards many human types (species) actually living at the same time, and intermarrying together. The "evolution" being uncovered is of the micro type, where people develop different bodies (short, tall, heavy, light), and other features typical within any biological group. No proof of macro-evolution has been uncovered from kind to kind (primate to human). *Science Illustrated,* in 2012, stated that extremely well-preserved entire skeletons that have not disintegrated in two million years, are laying on the surface of the ground. Obviously, if the DNA is still available, this means that the human fossils are actually all recent—meaning that many species existed together in the same time period—no millions of years for evolution. *Science News* in 2012, in an article: *"Tangled Roots,"* reported clear signs of inter-breeding of human types, and this conclusion was due to recovering DNA from various human types, supposedly hundreds of thousands of years old. This will require the dominant theory of human development to be revised. These scientists now conclude that there is a need to test the DNA from *bone* samples, from museum *fossils* (note these "fossils" are actually "bone" and still have DNA to test), from all over the world, of all these various human types, to determine just how we are all interrelated.

Science is quick to point out in textbooks, that the difference between primates and human DNA is only one percent. At first, this sounds like we are so close, that only a couple of mutations could possibly cause a human to be born to a primate. But, one percent is equal to *30 million* nucleotides, out of the three billion in the DNA structure. As of 2004, new evidence actually pointed to a three percent difference, not one percent. Dr. Tomkins (Ph.D. in Genetics from Clemson University), reported in 2013 that for the primary chimp chromosomes (autosomes), the amount of optimally aligned DNA sequence provided differences between 24-34 percent—nowhere near only one percent.

One of the "oldest" of human fossils, a skull #1470, discovered by Richard Leakey, theorized to be 2.8 million years old, actually looks more human than newer fossils (101—pg. 240-241).

Science News reports in 2014, that scientists have been forced to theorize the split from chimps to humans began much farther back in time—13 million years ago or more, now, due to lack of evidence to support *theories* of human evolution—the evidence is too elusive and the more we know about DNA makeup, the more changes are needed—thus the need for more time.

There clearly is no reason to accept, as *fact,* the theory that dinosaur bones, and other fossils, are millions of years old. As has already been shown, Carbon-14 dating, radiometric dating, and DNA methods are subject to many variables and assumptions about the geologic strata and their theorized ages, as proposed by scientists using paradigm A and long ages for evolution. Fossil evidence is found in several strata, even on the top of Mt. Everest, and all life forms are recorded in the fossil record, fully developed, and all in the same strata (all from the same age).

Many of the life forms in the world point to a common age. The oldest tree, the Bristle cone pine in Las Vegas, Nevada, dates to 2,590 B.C., and the ones in Israel date to 2,300 B.C. The Great Barrier Reef in Australia dates to 2,250 B.C. The oldest calendar in the world, the Chinese calendar, dates to 2,680 B.C. The Sahara Desert expands 4 miles each year, and dates to 2,250 B.C. The scholars who study the Bible place the great flood, which would have reset life timelines, roughly at 2,550 B.C. These dates all point toward a common beginning.

All this evidence supports the scientists using paradigm B and young age. They use only observable data, which points to catastrophic events and flooding, resulting in the variations in radiometric data, and also accounting for the evidence of fossils across the various strata and mountains. Additionally, these catastrophic events would account for the great extinctions of dinosaurs and other species.

Concerning evolution, in November 1992, Jeffery Levinton, Professor of Ecology and Evolution, at the State University of New York, in an article in *Scientific American* (72), wrote: "*A Cambrian explosion in animal diversity certainly did occur.*" Evolutionary biologists are still trying to determine why *no* new body plans have appeared during the past half a billion years. Attempts to find an answer with the tools of molecular biology have been inconclusive. Biologists postulate that the sequences of nucleotide bases in DNA and of amino acids in proteins mutate at approximately constant rates; the sequences can, therefore, be used as a kind of molecular clock. Evidence obtained by sequencing the 185 ribosomal RNA (molecules that aid in the synthesis of proteins), from various species suggests that many of the phyla appeared almost *simultaneously*.

Professor Levinton goes on to say: "*Just as all automobiles are fundamentally modeled after the first four-wheel vehicles, all the evolutionary changes since the Cambrian period have been mere variations on those basic themes. All in all, the facts still point to an explosion of complex life near the beginning of the Cambrian period. The actual extent of that explosion can be appreciated only by looking critically at the fossil record*" (72).

Chinese paleontologist, Hou Xian-quang, in separate fossil discoveries, in China, has reached the same conclusion: That all forms of life which exist today appear *suddenly* in the fossil record, fully developed, all at the *same time*, with no "links" having been found (74).

Scientists using paradigm B, place the age of the earth and life between 6,000 and 15,000 years old, based on evidence, much of which has been presented in this book. These include measurements of corrected Carbon-14 dates, correlated to account for early catastrophic events, earth and solar system magnetic data dating, fossil evidence of the sudden appearance of all species, fully developed, at the same time, with *no* missing links ever having been discovered, also measurements of coal, oil and gas formations and helium accumulation data, and many, many other areas already discussed.

Dr. Gish, professor of Natural Science, explains how all science agrees with the *Second Law of Thermodynamics,* which describes all natural processes as going from order to disorder—from complex to simple. Many scientists, however, still *believe* in the evolution of matter and life evolving from simple to complex (given enough time), even though the natural laws of science *disprove* this. The key word is "believe." The evidence says *no.*

The problem for life originating *naturally* is that science has discovered that DNA, proteins, RNA, and the cell are all required to develop *simultaneously.* None can exist without the other. Fred Hoyle, British Astronomer, and Francis Crick of the Salk Institute of Double Helix fame, have each suggested that life could not have begun without some unknown outside influence (space aliens).

DNA, which stores genetic information (the blueprints of life molecules), cannot function without proteins, and RNA molecules.

RNA (which transports the correct blueprints to the proper location site for life molecules), cannot function without proteins, DNA molecules, and a cell.

Proteins cannot function without DNA and RNA molecules.

A cell cannot survive without RNA molecules.

Dr. Francis Crick, Nobel Prize medalist in DNA, says there is *no* mathematical possibility of DNA occurring naturally. DNA is a binary 4-bit code, multiplied thousands of times. Life is intelligent software, not simply chemicals and elements. It takes *millions* of these 4-bit codes to make even a simple cell, much less a complex organism. There is actually more data encoded in the DNA of a single cell than there is data required to construct the space shuttle.

In 1999, in *Nature,* there are two references to mutations actually threatening life's survival, as opposed to the theory of mutations being a source of evolving. These were discussed by James F. Crow, Adam Eyre-Walker, and Peter D. Keightley. Their conclusions are that the harmful mutation rates in advanced species are extremely high. So high, in fact, that theories of species evolving in successive generations is highly doubtful, and calls into question any scientific evidence of life evolving through the process of mutations.

Early in 2008, Dr. Barney Maddox, referring to studies reported by J. Sanfore, in *Genetic Entropy and the Mystery of the Genome*, states that the underlying genetic mechanism of "evolution" is random mutation, and specifically mutation that is beneficial to life. Biology textbooks, in theory, present positive and negative mutations to students as though these were commonplace and roughly equal in number. However, these books fail to inform students that unequivocally *positive mutations are unknown* to genetics, since they have never been observed (or are so rare as to be irrelevant). The biology textbooks in *other* chapters teach that most mutations are pathologic, or disease-causing, but they don't apply that information to evolution. The worst diseases doctors treat today are caused by genetic mutations. Nearly 4,000 diseases are caused by mutations in DNA, according to *Medical Genetics: Principles and Practice*, by J. Nora. The ratio of "beneficial mutations" to harmful mutations is 0.00041. Thus, even if a very rare mutation could be "beneficial," the next 10,000 mutations in any evolutionary sequence would each be fatal or crippling, and each of the next 10,000 imaginary mutations would bring the evolution process to a halt.

Most scientists now agree that mutations destroy life. No *new* information is added during mutations, information is only scrambled. Flies are used by scientists to study mutation rates and possible evolution to other life forms, because of their prolific birth rates. Many generations of flies can be studied in a short amount of time. Scientists excuse the reason flies' offspring always die when they mutate, by explaining that flies have probably evolved to their highest state already.

Many Paradigm B biologists point to the subject of "irreducible complexity" as evidence that life forms cannot possibly evolve from one kind to another. Irreducible complexity states that all parts are needed for a life component to operate without dying. Like a mouse trap, you cannot remove one of the basic parts without eliminating its ability to work. This is true of basic parts in a cell also. If one part is removed, then it dies, meaning that all parts need to be in place *simultaneously*. In the flagellum, a hair-like appendage extending from a cell (one small part of a cell which allows the cell to maneuver), actually has 40 separate parts needed at the same time, or the flagellum is inoperative. Some scientists have countered with the theory called the "Co-opt Theory," where parts needed are borrowed from other already existing life forms, so that the "new" life form doesn't have to "make" all the parts at the same time. Of course the flagellum (again – only a small part of a cell), requires 30 parts which are *unique* to it alone.

Dr. Andrey Cherstvy of the Max Planck Institute for Physics of Complex Systems in Germany, along with Gary Vezzon of the Institute for Basic Sciences, have shown that electrostatic effect of DNA favor *like species* interaction over *different* species interaction. For decades now, the theory of evolution has relied upon the assumption that new information must be added into one species. Mutations have been proven to be overwhelmingly destructive, and therefore, only by some process of sharing of information has the theory of evolution been able to try and explain how the DNA structure can evolve with *new,* non-destructive information. It has been known for a long time now, that one of the mechanisms used by DNA sequences to link together is the attraction of these sequences to each other, due to their electrostatic charge, which is quite large. But, electrostatic charges of DNA sequences from different species have been shown to actually be repulsive to each other. Thus, sequences of DNA information from different species would never mix because their electrostatic charges would repulse each other.

It has become evident that there is *no* evidence for *Macro-* evolution. *Micro*-evolution however, does not require *"new"* information in order to change a species slightly, which we do see evidence of. But, macro-evolution, where large changes are needed with *"new"* information, in order to change one species into a different species, is not supported by any evidence—it is only a theory that this is how life must have come into being.

There are many races in the human species. Research done by J. Tennessen has shown that the *maximum* time needed for todays varied race populations would require 5,115 years for the diversity of the human genome we see today.

Studies released in 2006, in the February issue of "Newsweek," detail how science, using mDNA (mitochondrial DNA—DNA passed down to the females of a population), has been able to trace the path humans took after the first humans left their place of origin (*believed* to be East Africa/Western Sahara). This evidence matches the description given in the Bible of how people would have spread around the world after the flood of Noah's time (with one difference, of course, between the Bible and conventional science— *Time*). Under the biblical understanding, this all occurred over a period of 4,000 years, whereas, under the evolutionary theory, this occurred over a period of 80,000 years. The mDNA evidence is based on an assumption that mDNA mutates every 20,000 years. Of course, Ann Gibbons wrote in *"Science,"* in January 1998, in an article titled: *"Calibrating the Mitochondrial Clock,"* that the rate of decay is actually much faster, and the evidence indicates Eve traces back to about 6,000 years, not 80,000 (see the Globe Timeline Chart in the Appendix).

Scientific evidence reported in 2014 by Dr. Jeanson PhD., in cell biology at Harvard University shows mutation rates for mDNA show the age of humans, fruit flies, roundworms, and water fleas (which represent three phyla of life—Cordata, Arthropoda, and Nematoda), all to be within an age of 10,000 years—not millions or billions of years.

Further, Harvard University Anthropologist Philip Rightmire reports that new discoveries, in 2011, in a West Asian site called Dmanisi (which date older that African sites), suggest that man may have originated in Turkey, not in Africa as has always been presumed. This evidence was supported by geologist Reid Ferring, of the University of North Texas, as reported in the Proceedings of the National Academy of Sciences. Stone tools were found with the bone fragments in the Dmanisi area that pre-date fossils from Africa, suggesting that man spread from Turkey to Africa.

Ironically, this theory of man originating in Turkey agrees with the Bible, which records that mankind spread after the flood of Noah from Turkey. In 2013, archaeologists reported in *Biblical Archeological Review*, that in Turkey, a site called Gobekli Tepe has been dated to even pre-date the pyramids of Egypt. This is a massive site, with huge stones, and the animals carved in the stones are of animals not native to the area of Turkey, suggesting that at this early date, these animal kinds were in the area...perhaps, having left the ark?

So, who has the proof of *macro*-evolution? The biologist says that the geologist has it. The geologist says that the botanist has it. The botanist says that the anthropologist has it. The anthropologist says that science of radio-dating has it. And so it goes, with everyone trying to hold on to an old theory, with no verifiable evidence.

There is evidence to support an age for the earth and life of between 6,000 and 15,000 years. There is only *theory* to support ages of millions and billions of years.

LANGUAGE, RACE, AND AGE

See *Target Truth Ministries.com*
for News & Updates

There are two areas upon which scientists agree: language and race.

Language experts, in studying language data, note that *no* known language in *all* history was, in any sense, primitive (53). Even Sanskrit is more intricate and complicated than many contemporary languages (54). In fact, all languages seem to be going from a more complex form to an easier form, less complicated, and easier in which to communicate. In linguistics, this development is known as a movement from "synthetic" languages (highly inflected), to "analytic" language (discrete grammatical units) (78).

This is quite the opposite direction from how one might think a primitive language would evolve into today's language. Writings, in fact, since their beginnings less than 10,000 years ago, have moved from complexity to simplicity.

In Genesis 4:20-22, we read that in just seven generations, from Adam and Eve, people had already developed animal husbandry, music, and metallurgy, as well as language.

Another common feature of early language are references made by Sumerian writings, Assyrian tablets, Hebrew parchments, Chinese writings from 2400 B.C., Aztec and Inca stone writings, and others, to great flooding in their past. A catastrophic event that all these various ancient people share in their writings is of this great flooding. The Chinese writings include details which match the biblical account, including that the water came from *below* the earth, as well as from the sky. Also, the Chinese word for "boat," is a picture of a boat with eight people aboard (Noah's family on the ark totaled eight). E.A. Truax, in an article in *Acts & Facts,* in 1991, entitled: "Genesis According to the Miao People," reports that the ancient Chinese record *Feng-su T'ung-yi*, states that all people on earth are descended from "Nu-wa," considered an ancient version of the name Noah. James Legge in *The Notions of the Chinese Concerning God and Spirits*, in 1852, reports that the Book of History, the *Shu Jing*, records the Emperors proclamation of the annual "Border Sacrifice," which is very close to the biblical account. *"Heavenly Sovereign Shang Di (the one true God and Creator of the universe), states that in the beginning, there was the great chaos, without form and dark. The five planets had not begun to revolve, nor the sun, nor the moon to shine. In the midst thereof there existed neither forms nor sound. Thou, O Spiritual Sovereign, came forth in thy Presidency and did divide the grosser parts from the purer. Thou madest heaven, earth, and man. All things with reproductive power got their being."* The Chinese pictographs include many themes historic event recorded in Genesis 1-11. A Creator God...a heaven and earth...a garden...a man made from earth...temptation involving a tree...weeds and thorns representing punishment...a universal flood...a boat with 8 people...a confusion of tongues...and a seven day week. Also, the Chinese believed ancient humans lived for long periods of time, just as the early Greeks and Romans believed early humans lived for up to 1,000 years.

The Mayan calendar dates the flood to November of 2,370 B.C., per the *Diesden Codex*, which is a Mayan document from the period of the Toltecs of Mexico. The Chinese calendar begins about 2,680 B.C., around the same time the Bible records the flood of Noah. The Bible's rough date for the flood is sometime around 2,550 B.C., placing these various calendars within 200 years of the Bible's rough date.

In fact, 272 ancient written accounts from all over the world have been discovered, virtually all of which specify universal destruction by flooding (75, 76). Linguist, Dr. Charles Berlitz, Chinese

Pictograph Linguist, Dr. Ethel Nelson, and Arthur Custance make note of ancient writings from all parts of the world with reference to catastrophic flooding, including the Canadian and American Indians, in addition to the South American Indians, Egyptian writings in the tomb of Seti I, Hindu writings from India, the Koran, Chinese writings dating back to 2,400 B.C., and many, many more (76, 77). The American Hualapai Indians left ancient petroglyphs in the area of Davis Dam California (near the Colorado River), depicting a vessel carrying eight people, including the chief, across the flood waters (similar to the Chinese Pictograph). The Hualapai tradition closely resembles the story of Noah, per William Hoesch, M.S. Geology.

In 2013, archeology is reporting on a new discovery of a massive stone structure called Gobekli Tepe, in Turkey, which predates even the Great Pyramids of Egypt. It has animals carved into its stones of animals, not native to the Turkey area. Because Noah landed in Turkey, it is theorized that perhaps these animals were around this area, just after the flood, and then spread to climates more suitable.

It is interesting that language started out in a very complex form, but equally interesting, is how the written literature in each ancient language, refers to catastrophic flooding, and how this ties in with what we have just studied from geologic and fossil sources, which also point to great flooding, around 5,000 years ago (14, 17, 22, 24).

Currently, there is a worldwide study underway on the common ancestry of all languages. Linguists James Matisoff, of the University of California, Berkeley; Joseph Greenberg, of Stanford University; linguist Merritt Ruhlen and Vitaly Shevoroshkin, of the University of Michigan; Colin Renfrew, of the University of Cambridge; and Aharon Dolgopolsky, of the University of Haifa, are compiling evidence showing that originally, there was one language, and around 10,000 years ago, it is theorized that language split into various branches.

Ziggurats, massive towers built for the purpose of worship, have been found in numerous places in Mesopotamia as well as at Babylon. Near the a most incredible inscription has been found:

"The erection of this tower highly offended all the gods. In a night they threw down what man had built and impeded their progress. They were scattered abroad and their speech was strange."

Josephus quotes the Sibyl in *Antiquities*, book 1 chapter IV:3 concerning people being dispersed and language being confounded. Samuel Noah Kramer published a Sumerian tablet in *Journal of the American Oriental Society* which clearly states that at one time everyone spoke the same language.

Randall Isacc, executive director of American Scientific Affiliation (with over 1600 members), states that the original population began with a group of about 10,000—not a single pair of humans. He states that the genetic sequencing of the DNA we see today would require this size of a population base to begin with (141—see "people of Nod and Hebrew interpretation of Genesis").

DNA studies, reported in Science News in 2011, by geologist Reid Ferring, state that Turkey is being considered as the source of man, not Africa, as has always been presumed.

Scientists are in agreement in these areas of all races having come from a common human ancestry. Scientists also agree ancient writings were very complex, and come from one common source, and there is a common reference, from an overwhelming number of sources, in reference to catastrophic flooding all over the world.

New studies by Luigi Gavalli-Sforza, of Stanford University, in DNA sample comparisons of various ethnic groups, are verifying the common link between language and historical DNA groupings of various human populations. In 2012, science reported in a report by J. Tennessen, titled: "Evolution and functional impact of rare coding variation from deep sequencing of human exomes," that the maximum likelihood for the current diversity of genes in human population groups is 5,115 years—perhaps pointing to Noah?

For a long time, misconceptions revolved around the various races, but now scientists agree we all descended from a shared common ancestry. There were misconceptions about skin color, and features such as slanted or round eyes. It is now known that the difference in eyes is simply a result of how much fat is retained around the eye, a genetic feature. And, skin color is simply a genetic trait also, relating to how much melanin, which all humans have, our cells produce. In fact, it has been proved, long ago, that it would be possible for an entire range of skin color, from very white to very black, to be produced by a human couple in only *one* generation.

Science tells us, that today, the entire population can change in 2,000 years. Light-skinned people produce little melanin, and dark-skinned people can produce lots. In sunny areas, sunlight produces skin cancer for light-skinned people, while darker skin limits the sunlight to just enough to produce vitamin D, and thus, protect the person. In colder areas, dark skin would not allow enough light to produce vitamin D, resulting in rickets, whereas, light-skinned people receive more light, allowing ample production of vitamin D.

Dr. Henry Morris noted years ago that estimates of population growth show the human population we witness today, could develop from one set of humans easily within *no* more than about 6,000 years (73). Morris points out that worldwide population growth rate is about two percent per year. Morris said if we assume it would have been much less than that in the past, several times less, say only half a percent, then the present world population would have developed in *only 4,000 years*. If one were to assume longer time periods, even allowing for growth rates several times smaller than present day rates, the population of the world would equal the number of molecules in the entire planet. If people have been inhabiting the planet for three million years (even longer as evolution suggests), there should be 150,000 people per square inch today. Obviously, the human population hasn't been around all that long.

At the time of the Tower of Babel (Genesis 11), it is estimated that the earth's population would have been around 250,000. In the years after the flood, there was longevity, better genetics, low mortality, less environmental damage, and God was blessing the replenishment of the earth. At the time of the construction of the pyramids of Giza (conventional dating), there would have been around three million people in Egypt. This is the number estimated that would be needed to support Egypt while the pyramids were being constructed (one million needed just for the overall construction). At the time of Moses, 1,000 years later, it is estimated that the population of Egypt was about five to six million, including about one-and-a-half million Israelites. At the time of Jesus, the population of the world is estimated to be around 200 million.

Ever wonder about how humans could live so long, as written about in the Bible, in Genesis, even up to 1,000 years? Michio Kaku, New York University, reported in 2008, on how Nobel Prize biologist Paul Nurse, established that humans are not genetically programmed to die. There are no genes for aging. We die because cells accumulate damage over time, due to cosmic radiation and free radical activity within the cell, and the repair process cannot keep up. Genetic biologists, Dr. Gordon Lithgow and Dr. Judith Campisi, from the Buck Institute for Age Research in California, report that genes already exist within our genetic make-up to extend life by enhancing the repair process, and that humans should be able to live 1,000 years or more. Cambridge biologist, Aubrey De Grey, is pursuing research to reverse aging by aggressive gene repair. Guess the Bible wasn't so far-fetched after all. Early humans had undamaged genes, and after several generations, these genes became damaged (141). Ancient texts from the Sumerians, Egyptians, Greeks, and Romans all tell of people living to between 800 and 1,000 years—not just the Bible.

Urana Clarke wrote: *"How our Music Began,"* in the *Book of Knowledge*, Vol. 18, and she tells us that music also shows either a common origin, or a *worldwide* cultural interaction in ancient times, when such communication was considered impossible. The music scales we use today, are the same as those used over 4,000 years ago in various parts of the world, from China, to the American Indians, to Greece etc. (101 — pg. 61-62). In 2008, Fazale Rana reports that in Germany, archeologists discovered a flute, which dates to the very beginning of humanity, crafted from solid ivory, with finger holes at intervals to produce different tones—again more evidence of "ancient" stone-age peoples with very "modern" tools and techniques.

Here again, there is a variety of evidence to put the beginnings of humans around 6,000 to 15,000 years ago, but there is no proof, fossil or living, of millions and billions of years for the age of life and our earth, only theories.

As we move on to the final sections, we are still at a loss to explain why the greatest of all the seven wonders of the world, the great pyramids, are *totally* missing from the greatest of all historical books, the Bible. These great structures are the focus of science, astronomy, math, culture and anthropology. The Bible has hundreds of references to Egypt and the pharaohs, both in the old and new testaments, but one *never* finds even a hint of the pyramids. Why?

CIVILIZATIONS
THE QUEEN OF HEAVEN

The Moon Goddess
See *Target Truth Ministries.com*
for News & Updates

R evelation 17:5 refers to all false teachings when it refers to "The Great Harlot," the false religion, or worldly type of church.

What is the *mystery*? Why *Babylon*? Who is the *woman*?

The cultic worship of mother, child, and fertility, goes back to the earliest writings. From the very beginning (even in Genesis 10:8-10), one finds reference to the beginnings of this false worship, with the reference to Nimrod (who, with Semiramis and her son, Tammuz), have fostered many forms of cultic worship through the centuries based upon God's story in the Zodiac. These include Anu and Ishtar birthing Tammuz at the time of Israel (Jer. 7:18, 44:17-19, 25), and they lead eventually to Egypt with Osiris and Isis (the cosmic mother), birthing Horus, the Egyptian copy of Tammuz.

These mythical deities were all based on rites of fertility, and even today, many celebrate Easter as "a season of fertile spring-time." In ancient Samaria, this spring celebration involved the exchanging of Ishtar (Easter) eggs. Further, the son of this goddess (Tammuz), was "resurrected to life" in these mythical legends. As one looks through history, one finds numerous "imitations" of

God's plan which puts, either some person (such as Nimrod), or this world, or Satan, at the center of attention, instead of God.

Whether one is Christian, Mormon, Jehovah's Witness, Jewish, Muslim, or any faith, God tells us the only path to God's kingdom is by trusting in Jesus. Jesus claimed He alone is the way (John 14:6). Jesus gave us eyewitness evidence of His power over death (1 Cor. 15:1-8; Acts 1:1-8), and Jesus welcomes all who will trust in Him. Many Protestants, Catholics, a few Muslims, a few Jewish, and others, have put their trust in Jesus, and they will all be welcomed into the kingdom of heaven. There are also many who call themselves Catholic, or Protestant, who are not truly "born again" (John 3:3-6), and even though they think of themselves as pretty good people (go to church, etc.), their priority in this life is not Jesus. Jesus Himself said that they will not be welcome in God's kingdom (Matt. 7:21-23, 25:1-13). The key to the kingdom of God is trusting in Jesus.

In the ancient world, the mythical deities were first defined by the Sumerians (Babylon – people of the East). The Sumerians, the first literate civilization, worshiped the moon goddess, which was called by many names, including Nanna, and Suen. This was the dominant goddess of the Fertile Crescent. Later on, the Akkadians (Semite peoples), took the name Suen, and transliterated it to "Sin." Thus, Sin became the favorite name for the moon goddess throughout the ancient Fertile Crescent. From the very beginning, the crescent moon was the symbol of the moon goddess (female). Sin is also viewed as a male in other areas and at different periods of time, as will be explained in the following pages.

Later still, the Egyptians would become the defining force, followed by Greece, with its capital at Babylon, and then Rome, at the time of Christ. All these empires had their mythology rooted in these Babylonian (eastern) deities, and the moon goddess (god) Sin.

In the city of Ur (Abraham's home), ancient tablets list the primary deities as An (the male god), and Inanna, or Nammu (the Queen of Heaven) (103—pg. 189-190). The Stella of Ur-Nammu (the female goddess – Queen of Heaven), has the crescent moon placed at the very top of the register of gods, because the moon goddess was the highest of gods, not the male. Even in Egypt, in the old kingdom, the great mother god (Isis—the cosmic mother), was revered as deity. In fact, in the old kingdom temple, only the great mother has a column dedicated to her as deity—no males are listed. Centuries later, in Egypt, the male would dominate.

In the Sumerian (Babylonian/eastern) mythology, the origin of the whole universe was due to Nammu, the water goddess (104—pg. 303). From her waters was birthed all we see, including all the male gods. This is an imitation of God's creation where the "waters" were divided (Gen. 1:6-8). One of these births was to the moon goddess Sin (104—pg. 74). In Mesopotamia, the female goddess figure was dominant, until animal husbandry and domestication later became established. Only then, did the male god figure begin to dominate in some cultures. But, in Mesopotamia, where Abraham came from, the pagan male gods were still a servant to the Mother Goddess of all creation. The Mother Goddess was considered unmarried, and in some locations, a virgin. It was the reproductive power of the earth, which was associated with the Mother Goddess (Mother Earth), and which was of paramount importance in agricultural life in the ancient world.

As agriculture became controllable, the male dominance of heavenly deities took hold. Sin came to be seen as a male moon god, which became later known as Al-ilah (the highest of gods) in the Arab world, hundreds of years after Christ. Even so, Sin still retained a female form (Al-lat – the female moon goddess). In the Sumerian (eastern) explanation of gods, a god could also be a goddess (103—pg. 193)...this has confused scholars for centuries. But, the origin of this male female change can be cleared up by studying the Greek (western) myth. The Greek empire, which came much later, and which established its capital at Babylon, has given us better records of their mythical deities origins, and how this moon god (male) could be also known as a moon goddess (Queen of Heaven).

All this mythology is a product of perverting (imitating) God's Word from the very beginning. Genesis 2:21-24 tells us how God first created man (Adam), and then "out of man," God made woman (Eve/the bearer of life). In the Greek myth, Zeus (equivalent of Adam), produces Hera, the female goddess. Hera is not born to

Zeus, but she comes "out of him" (just as Eve comes out of Adam). Therefore, in the ancient Babylonian myths, a god could become a goddess. In the Greek myth, Hera became known as Athena *after a great flood* (Noah?). Athena, the mother goddess, is usually pictured with the serpent. The serpent is central to mythology in *all* ancient cultures *all* over the world, due to the fact that, as in the Greek understanding, it was the serpent who gave man knowledge, which was previously restricted to only God (Gen. 3:1-5). This is the perversion (imitation) of God's Word. The Sumerians (at Babylon), began a false worship where the serpent became the source of knowledge, and worship was given to the serpent, and to the moon goddess, the bearer of life.

All of this Greek myth is actually rooted in Babylon, the capital of the Greek Empire at the time of Alexander the Great.

In the Greek (western) understanding, the moon god Sin (male), became transformed to a female goddess, and became the highest of gods. This was brought about in mythology as the result of the earth goddess Inanna becoming the Queen of Heaven (as well as the Queen of Earth), due to her marrying many other gods, including Anu (the primary male god) (104—pg. 78, 86). She became the moon goddess with resurrection power, thus, replacing the male moon god Sin. Later still, the moon goddess was once again viewed as a male (Al-ilah – the highest of gods), at the time of Mohammad, 600 years after Christ.

As the Sumerian origins gave way to the Semitic culture, these deities' male names became (depending upon the area of the world one lived in), Nimrod, Marduk, Assur, and Ba'al. The female names became Semiramis, Inanna, Ishtar, Astarte, and Ba'al-Ti. Many of them had a child called Tammuz. Tammuz, son of Inanna (Semiramis, Ishtar, Astarte, etc.), was considered a god. He was supposedly resurrected in these myths, after his death, but he was always the earthly servant of the Mother Goddess of the universe. The Assyrian counterpart of Inanna was Ishtar, the Queen of Heaven and Earth. The Queen of Heaven, and the Mother of Earth was the dominant deity, due to her acts of renewal and regeneration.

The kings of Mesopotamia were often regarded as subservient to the goddess because (unlike Egypt, with its predictable cycle of flooding for agriculture, which the kings could predict), the river waters in Mesopotamia were unpredictable—indicating the kings had no power. Thus, all worship was directed to the Queen of Heaven, who was also the Mother of Earth—not the male kings, or their male deities.

The Bible's Old Testament rebuked the worship of the moon god (Deut. 4:19, 17:3; 2 Kings 21:3, 5, 23:5; Jer. 8:2, 19:13; Zeph. 1:5, etc.).

Over time (as men gained control over agriculture and animal husbandry), the sky god (the sun), was seen as the greater, more powerful of gods—controlling seasons, and weather, and war. However, the Mother Goddess, being associated with the moon, as well as the earth, was still venerated as a source of life and rebirth.

As time progressed, the moon goddess, combined with Isis (from Egypt), and became known as Namaia (104—pg. 80, 86). Eventually, male dominance caused a return to the worship of the moon as a male god (Sin) once again. In time, Sin became Al-ilah (a title meaning "highest deity"). Montgomery Watt, in the *Journal of Semitic Studies* (Vol. 16, "Belief in a High God in Pre-Islamic Mecca"), states that this moon god/goddess, was the primary god of Ur, where Abraham lived (around 2,000 B.C.). Nabonidus (555-539 B.C. – over a thousand years before Muhammad), the last king of Babylon, built Tayma, Arabia, as a center of moon god worship. The Arab tribes always remained steadfast in worship of the moon god, Al-ilah. In fact, Mecca was built as a shrine for the moon god.

At the time of Mohammad (around 600 A.D.), this moon god Sin (male), was seen as married to the sun goddess. Three stars of heaven were his daughters: Al Lat, Al-Uzza, and Monat...all considered high gods. The moon god was *named* Sin, and his *title* was Al-ilah (the highest god), which became Allah. Muhammad declared that Allah was not only the greatest god, but the only god. This was due to a vision Muhammad received that the main god of his city (Al-ilah – the moon god), was the one, true god (symbolized by the crescent moon today, by Islam, as well as the Wicca, and Mother Earth faiths (143, 144).

To this day, the Muslim faithful fast during the month which begins and ends with the appearance of the crescent moon in the sky.

Centuries later, in Egypt, the ancient Tammuz myth becomes the story of Osiris, Isis, and their son Horas. Many ancient myths, including the Tammuz myth, seem to parallel the story of Christ (virgin birth, resurrection etc.). These myths were elevated to historical status in the late 1800's and the early 1900's. Recent scholarship has, however, shown each of these myths fall far short of being historic parallels. Lee Strobel (131) has provided evidence showing these myths have been either later embellished to relate to Christ, or were actually created after the time of Christ. Historically these myths in no way even closely relate to the life of Christ. We must remember the original story of the virgin, and the resurrection, were given in the Zodiac by God, and it has been perverted into these other myths (see Zodiac Study at Target Truth Ministries .com).

After the time of Christ, all the variations of the Mother Goddess, the Queen of Heaven, whether called Ishtar in Mesopotamia, or Asherah, Anat, or Astarte in Syria, or Isis in Egypt (Isis actually means "She of many names"), all of these had formed into the universal female goddess, a beautiful virgin, generally known as "The Queen of Heaven."

Today, supernatural apparitions of a glowing woman (a bright light), are occurring at increasing intervals, all over the world. The last fifty years has seen an explosion in these appearances. The apparition claims to be "Mary, Mother of God," and she speaks through people, sometimes through several people, at the same time. *These apparitions have been documented*, and in some cases, recorded on film. Millions of people worldwide now claim to have witnessed the apparition. These signs, wonders, and miracles, are causing mass conversions, and life-changing experiences.

Jesus also performed signs and wonders, and eyewitness evidence of these are given in the Bible (such as changing water to wine, and walking on water, etc.). Jesus also fulfilled over 300 prophecies, written hundreds of years before His birth, as recorded in the Old and New Testaments by actual eyewitnesses.

- The Mary apparition claims signs and wonders, such as changing silver to gold, and in fact, many such instances have been *testified to, and recorded.*

Jesus *healed* many, and raised people from the dead, and eyewitness testimony is given of these miracles in the Bible.

- The Mary apparition claims to heal people, and, in fact, *many healings have been documented*, and recognized by various churches, including the Roman Catholic Church.
  In John 14, Jesus said that He was the way, the truth, and the life, and that no one would enter the kingdom of heaven, but by Him.
- The Mary apparition asks people to read their Bible, pray every day, trust in Jesus, and she says she has been appointed by the Father, and her Son, to save all nations, bring unity to all the faiths, and global peace.

Peace – Love – Unity. All is great…but, is it?

The last two popes (including the current pope, in 2013), as well as many other Roman Catholic leaders, in light of these great signs, wonders, and miracles, have formally dedicated the *entire* world to Mary. They are trusting in her to bring unity between all faiths, as well as global peace. This is because Jesus is too controversial and divisive (Jesus is a judge, and will divide and separate – Luke 12:49-53), and He did *not* come to bring peace.

God tells us to test all things (1 Thessalonians 5:21).

The apparition of Mary says she is the *mediator and intercessor*, between God and us. The Roman Catholic Church has proclaimed Mary as "intercessor." In 1854, she was declared "Mary, the conqueror of death and evil."
Hebrews 7:25 – Jesus is our Mediator/Intercessor.
1 Timothy 2:5 – There is one God, and one mediator (Jesus).

The apparition of Mary says she is our *advocate*, sent by the Father and Son.

1 John 2:1 – Jesus is our advocate.

Luke 1:47-48 – Mary called Jesus her God and Savior.

The apparition of Mary says she has been sent to *save the world*. She says she, alone, is able to *redeem* us, and the world. She describes herself as the *"ark of salvation."* The Roman Catholic Church declared Mary as the "Ark in Heaven" in 1950.

1 Peter 1:18-19 – Jesus is our Redeemer.

John 14:6 – Jesus only.

Luke 1:38 – Mary says she is the Lord's servant.

Acts 4:11-12 – Jesus only.

Hosea 13:4 – God only.

The apparition of Mary says she is ever-present to receive our prayers, and intercede for us. She is omnipresent. She is a co-redemptorist, able to redeem us *apart* from Jesus. The Roman Catholic Church is very close to proclaiming her the co-redemptorist. On August 16th 2007, the Pope said: *"Mary's glorification in her virginal body is the confirmation of her total solidarity with the Son, both in the conflict, and in victory...she is from all eternity... one and the same decree of predestination...the noble associate of the divine Redeemer...as Queen, she sits in splendor at the right hand of her Son."*

John 14:6 – No one but Jesus.

Isaiah 47:4 – The Lord is our Redeemer.

Isaiah 45:22 – One God – no other (Isa. 45:5-6, 44:6-8; 1 Cor. 8:4).

Acts 4:11-12 – Jesus only.

Luke 11:27-28 – Jesus said others as blessed as Mary.

The apparition of Mary says she atones for our sins, and suffers for us (as her heart, and Christ's heart, are one—and they suffer together for the world's sins). In 1950, the Roman Catholic Church proclaimed that Mary had gone to heaven as Jesus had – the "Assumption of Mary."

John 19:30 - Jesus said, "It is finished."

1 Peter 3:18 – Christ suffered once for all.

Hebrews 10:12-14, 18 – One sacrifice – no longer any suffering.

The apparition of Mary claims to be sinless—an immaculate conception, and to have ascended bodily into heaven, and is seen now as the "Bright and Morning Star." She will crush the serpent. The Roman Catholic Church proclaimed Mary as a perpetual virgin in 553 A.D., and proclaimed Mary an "Immaculate Conception," and "sinless" in 1854.

2 Corinthians 11:14-15 – Satan is an angel of light.

Romans 3:23 – All are sinners (Mary also).

Acts 1 – Jesus ascended, bodily, into heaven.

Genesis 3:15 – Jesus will crush the serpent.

Revelation 22:16 – Jesus is called the "Bright and Morning Star."

Isaiah 42:8 – God will give His glory to no one.

Isaiah 44:6 – God is the first and the last, beside God there is no other.

The apparition of Mary says statues and shrines are to be erected to her, and to be honored, and venerated, as a reminder of her presence. A statue is under construction now, which will be twice as tall as the Statue of Liberty. Mary was proclaimed "Mother of God" in 431 A.D., and named the "Queen and Gate to Heaven," in 1854, by the Roman Catholic Church.

Deuteronomy 4:14-19 – No idols, no statues, no heavenly wonders are to be worshiped.

Isaiah 42:8 – God will give His glory to no one.

The apparition of Mary often appears with a baby.

1 Peter 3:21-22 – Jesus was bodily resurrected as a *man*, not as a baby. He is now alive as the God-Man.

The apparition of Mary says she is to be called the Queen of Heaven, Mother of God, Queen of the Ages, the Lady of all Nations. She says when she is declared by the church to be co-redemptorist, that she will bring unity under one holy church, and peace to the world. The Roman Catholic Church has declared her the "Lady of All Nations" in 2005, in addition to all the other names, and is expected to proclaim her co-redemptorist in the near future.

1 Thessalonians 5:2-3 – Peace—then sudden destruction.
Daniel 8:25 – Peace—then destruction.
Daniel 9:27 – A peace covenant—then destruction.
Revelation 6:1-4 – A white horse (peace), then a red horse (war).
Daniel 7:23 – Unity of the nations, but devoured.
Revelation 13:7-8 – Unity, to be followed by death.
Revelation 17:18 – Unity, under a false religion.
Revelation 18:3 – Unity, under a false religion which is doomed.
2 Timothy 3:13 – Imposters will deceive.
2 Thessalonians 2:9-10 – The lawless one, with counterfeit signs and wonders, will deceive those who refuse the truth.
Matthew 24:24 – False prophets with great signs and wonders, (such as to deceive the very elect), will arise.
Galatians 1:8-9 – Reject even an angel who does not agree with God's Word.
2 Corinthians 11:14-15 – Satan is an angel of light.
1 Timothy 4:1 – In the end times, some will follow deceitful spirits.

How is it possible for Mary, the Queen of Heaven, to be the Lady of Nations, and to bring global peace, and bring unity to all faiths in the world (including Islam, and Buddhism, and Hinduism, etc.)?

It turns out that, just as it is described in God's Word (Jer. 7:18, 44:17-25; Ezek. 8:14), concerning the Queen of Heaven (who was worshiped going back as far as 4,000 years ago in Mesopotamia), this same "Mother of All Nations" has been venerated by many nations for all these years, (with the exception of those who follow the Bible). Of course, today, even many of those who call themselves Christian, have begun to accept the Queen of Heaven as the way to unity and global peace, including the largest Christian organization in the world—the Roman Catholic Church.

What about Islam? Chapter 19 of the Koran (Qur'an), is actually named after Mary. Islamic tradition is that Jesus is to have said that Allah has exhorted Him (Jesus), to honor His mother, who purged Him of vanity and wickedness. In chapter 21 of the Koran, Allah says he breathed into Mary his spirit, to make her a sign to all mankind. Islam venerates Mary as a pure and holy saint (even above Muhammad), whereas, the Koran says Muhammad must ask for forgiveness for his sins.

Apparitions of Mary have, in fact, appeared to millions of Muslims, and they have experienced healings, and they are in ever-increasing numbers making pilgrimages to Mary shrines in Iraq, Syria, Egypt, Turkey, and others. In chapter 66 of the Koran, Allah said he gives Mary as the faithful example for all the world's believers to follow.

It is the hope of the Pope, in Rome, as well as many others, that Islam will join Catholics in unity, under the veneration of Mary. To this end, the Roman Catholic Church has declared that the god of Islam is the *same* God recognized by the Roman Catholic Church. (143, 144).

How about Hindus, Buddhists, Taoists, and others, including faiths of the New Age, and even Wicca?

The primary deities of all these world religions has always included veneration of a female goddess, commonly called the Queen of Heaven, or Mother of Earth. This goddess is loved, because she is a goddess of life and birth, and she transcends nations and prejudices. She is welcomed by all nations, because her message is global peace, unity, and tolerance.

One of the most unexpected developments since the birth of Christ 2,000 years ago, is the rebirth today of the religion of the Queen of Heaven, the Mother Goddess. Buddhists revere and adore a female figure, which dates back to early times in India.

The Hindu faith has always revered the female goddess. The Chinese goddess is known as Kwan-yin (the Goddess of Mercy), who brings the faithful to heaven. In Japan, she is known as the goddess Kwan-on (the Mother of Mercy). In Japan, even converted Christians accept that their Kwan-on, is in fact, the foreshadowing of the goddess Mary.

The apparition of Mary is documented to have said that she has appeared in many forms, to many people, in different places.

So, it turns out that peoples of all nations are being won over to the peace, love, and unity, promised by the Queen of Heaven. *All, but one.* Notice, that one nation in all the world has, and does, treat the Queen of Heaven as evil wickedness (especially since in their history, they, too, once worshiped her, and they suffered for that worship). Now it becomes clear why Israel and Jerusalem, are a trouble to all the world (Zech. 12:1-9, 14:1-3). Furthermore, any nation which supports Israel, will be in direct opposition to the apparition, and to her followers, the nations of the world, who desire peace and unity.

The history of the Queen Mother has common threads for all nations from the beginning of recorded history, going all the way back to Jericho, the oldest of cities.

<u>Babylon</u> had a Mother Goddess cult. A primary god, Anu (a male), was god over the entire universe. But, he shared power with the Mother Goddess Nammu. She was credited with actually creating the universe for him to govern. Eventually Nimrod (Gen. 10:8-9), established himself as a god on earth, and after his death, was called Baal (the sun god). Nimrod's wife Semiramis, became the moon god with rebirth powers (seen as moon cycles). Certain religious practices, which began in Babylon, spread to all nations, and are with us even today in the Christian church (see *Birth of Christ* section). The Greek myths derive from these Babylonian roots (Babylon was the capital of the Greek Empire), and they have preserved a record for us of how these mother-child cults relate to God's creation, the fall, and the serpent. Man embraced the serpent as the provider of knowledge (see Greece). Ancient Mesopotamian clay tablets tell us their creator-god was depicted as a serpent (the god of knowledge).

<u>Jericho</u> had a goddess cult, a Mother Goddess deity. Archeologists have uncovered much evidence of this in the form of statues and figurines they place at 7,000 B.C.

<u>Nineveh</u> also had a female deity figure venerating maternity, a Mother Goddess.

Iraq, from which Abraham came, had a temple dedicated there to the Mother Goddess Inanna-Ishtar, and her son Dumazi-Tammuz, as far back as 3800 B.C.

Iran and Elam also had a female goddess statue on the Acropolis, dating to 3000 B.C.

Jericho, around 3000 B.C., was venerating skulls, and had linked the Mother Goddess to the land of the dead, and Mother Earth.

Egypt, around 2000 B.C., worshiped Seth, as the son of the earth god and the sky goddess. Egypt worshiped the sun god as the sustainer of life, but also worshiped the sky goddess as the producer of life, and also of reproduction. During the old kingdom, the great mother goddess was the primary deity — seen as the Milky Way (the cosmic mother) giving birth to the stars (the gods above).

Mesopotamia saw many transitions in their gods, until their primary gods of worship finally consolidated and became: A) Sin (the *moon* god/goddess — usually female, but sometimes male, depending on the local culture), B) Shamash (the sun god — male), and C) Adad (the storm god — male). The most important of these was the moon goddess — the crescent moon.

Greece as early as 1000 B.C., worshiped the Queen of Heaven, Athena, who was given authority by the serpent. Athena was worshiped as mother of all. Greek myth states Kronos (Chronos, or *time*), and Rhea (*earth*), united to form the first man Zeus (similar to Adam's creation by God — *One outside of time*, forming Adam from the dust, or *earth*). In the Greek myth, Hera comes out of Zeus (similar to Eve coming out of Adam). This is Satan's imitation of the Genesis creation, except that the Greeks worship the serpent, who gave man knowledge to become gods themselves. Later, the goddess Hera, reappears *after a great flood* as Athena, and she receives power from the serpent. Athena and the serpent are worshiped by the Greek Empire as the mother goddess. This Athena (goddess of the serpent), is given authority over the Sphinx,

a winged lion with the head of a *woman* (see *Zodiac* section—
Egyptian pyramid reference in next pages). The wings represent
power over the heavens, the lion represents power over the earth,
and the woman represents power over life.

Many cultures in ancient history had stories they passed down
through the centuries concerning the woman of heaven (a virgin),
as well as her child (and his death, and resurrection), and the judgment, and salvation of humankind.

In the oldest book in the Bible (Job 38:32—2150 B.C.), considered by many to be the oldest book in human history, there is
the reference to the Mazzaroth (Hebrew for constellations of the
Zodiac), as well as several individual constellations. Zodiac means
"the way" or *"the path,"* in Hebrew and in Sanskrit. In other words,
a picture of the way of salvation.

In all the ancient nations, the *same* 12 constellations, in the
same order, with the *same* pictures, are referenced as far back
in antiquity as we can go (142, 143). There must be a common
source (144).

It has been pointed out by scholars (including the historian
Josephus), that the original source for the Zodiac is God's gospel.
It was given to Adam and Eve, and passed down thru the genera-
tions of Noah, to the seventy nations. In the Arabic tradition, these
signs in the heavens are said to have come from Seth and Enoch.
Genesis 1:14 states that God gave us the stars for signs: Twelve
constellations, twelve tribes, twelve apostles (see also Rev. 12:1).
God named the stars (Ps. 147:4; Isa. 40:26). But, it is also noted that
God's gospel story in the heavens has been perverted, just as the
Bible today is being perverted by many. The term "seventh heaven"
(used by Islam and many others), refers to the five planets, the sun,
and the moon, each forming a crystal sphere, with the earth at the
center (2nd century, Ptolemy). The Bible refers to a third heaven
(2 Cor. 12:2).

When one looks at the Zodiac, one may question where to start
in this story in the heavens, because all the constellations are in
a circle. By going to the oldest Zodiacs, one of which is found in
the Egyptian temple of Esneh, 4,000 or more years old, the Sphinx

pictured there, points out where to start. The Sphinx head (a woman's head—see Greece in previous discussion), is toward Virgo, the virgin, and the tail toward Leo, the lion. Modern astrology has perverted the Zodiac, and it now begins with Aries, the lamb.

Throughout the history of these ancient cultures, there is a common reverence of a life-producing Mother Goddess. She was the dominant figure in the ancient Near Eastern religions. All of these cultures share a common source for worshiping her: namely, the Zodiac. However, if one actually studies the ancient names given by God to the individual stars and constellations, it becomes clear that the original story in the stars actually agrees with the message in the Bible, and these names for individual stars do not agree with the various other stories told by other ancient cultures.

Israel was forbidden by God to worship the Queen of Heaven. However, King Ahab became a worshiper, because of his wife Jezebel, and her priests of Ba'al. Archeological evidence shows that soon after Solomon's time, the Astarte sanctuary (the center of the goddess cult), stood next to the temple of the God of Israel (Jer. 7:18, 44:17-25; Ezek. 8:14).

John, in Revelation 12, gives us a picture of a woman (symbolic of the betrothed to God—the bride—all the host of heaven, some of which became Israel), bringing forth a Savior (Jesus). The woman is standing on the moon (the moon under her feet), meaning that Sin is conquered (see *Birth of Christ* section).

God's Word warns us about the Queen of Heaven.........

Isaiah 47:1-7 – A virgin queen of nations – daughter of Babylon.
Revelation 18:3-7 – A queen of all the nations – wicked.
Isaiah 47:9-11 – The queen will meet her end. Note that the false prophet will be eliminated by the beast in the very end. The beast will exalt himself (Rev.17:16; Dan. 11:45).
Zechariah 5:5-11 – A wicked woman in Babylon.
Revelation 18:2-3 – Wicked Babylon, a woman.
Revelation 2:20 – The harlot Jezebel is tolerated, which is a sin to God.

1 Kings 16:31-33 – Jezebel worships the Queen of Heaven, called Asherah.

Daniel 11:36-37 – Desire to worship the Queen of Heaven. The desire of people for the woman queen.

2 Thessalonians 2:3-12 – Before the day of the Lord's return, apostasy comes first—the mystery of lawlessness, which is already working in the world with signs, wonders, and deceptions, for those who do not love the truth.

Isaiah 47 – The wicked woman hides (v. 10). A mystery. Judged in the end times.

Zechariah 5:6-11 – The wicked woman is hidden. Hidden until the end-times. One ephah holds evil. Three measures, or pecks, equals one ephah (Matt. 13:33).

Revelation 17 – The wicked woman is the mystery of Babylon, a great harlot—false religion.

Matthew 13:33 – Evil is hidden by the woman. The whole world is corrupted (leavened). Three measures, or pecks, equals one ephah, which is supposed to be the offering to God, but it is leavened (puffed up – not pure – defiled – Zech. 5:6-7).

1 Thessalonians 5:21 – Test all things.

References (103 to 112)

The Queen of Heaven is a perversion of God's plan by Satan. It was God's plan that through Noah, *all* should know God's plan, the plan of redemption/reconciliation originally told in the Zodiac.

In Genesis, chapters 10 through 25, the families/ tribes/ generations are described, and from these names, we can understand who the present day nations are that the prophets describe in their writings. Example: Magog in the Hebrew, is Scythian in the Greek (Col. 3:11), is Russia and northern Turkey all the way to the wall of China today (144).

The Great Pyramids of Egypt are the *first* ones built in Egypt (possibly even before the flood of Noah), and false religions are established (141, 143). See Josephus, *Jewish Antiquities* i.2.

Nimrod of Babylon, almost immediately after the generations begin, establishes *the* major source of today's false religions (Rev. 17:1-7).

MYSTERY OF BABYLON/MOTHER OF HARLOTS ABOMINATION OF THE EARTH........goes back to the worship of the Mother God, Queen of Heaven, who became the Moon God named SIN. Mohammed proclaimed the Moon God Sin (called the greatest god Al-ilah), as the one true God, Allah. Sin (Allah), was also the main god of Abraham's father, being the main god of the city of Ur, where Abraham came from (thus, the phrase "the god of Abraham").

Abraham was chosen by God to fulfill God's plan of sharing God's Word of redemption/reconciliation to *all* the world through the generations of Abraham. Jesus Christ was to be born to these generations. It has always been God's plan to save souls, to give the plan of redemption/reconciliation to *every* soul. Satan's plan is to imitate God's plan with a false worship that looks like God's plan.

From Abraham, comes Jacob, later to be called Israel (Gen. 32:28), and God gives us a picture of His plan through the dream of Jacob called "Jacob's Ladder," where souls are seen coming to earth to be redeemed/reconciled, so they can return to God (141, 143). Also, from Abraham come the Arab nations, many of which adopt the religion of Islam, but not all. There are millions of Christian Arab peoples. Islam is not to be confused with Arab. Islam is the religion founded by Mohammed, but is really the result of the generations of Abraham not all following the one, true God, the Creator, Christ.

God's Word is not in conflict with any proof that science has in regards to creation, origins, and age. There is only conflict concerning some of the theories (see the *Science* section).

- Science says there was only one giant land mass called Pangaea originally (see the *Global Time Chart* in the Appendix).
- God's Word says, in Genesis 1:9, the land (singular) was formed.

- <u>Science</u> has given up on the "spark of life" theory today, and now prefers the life from "outer space" theory, and another theory with no proof (evolution), to explain humans today.
- <u>God's Word</u> says, in Genesis 1:28, that He created humans.
- <u>Science</u> theorizes that the one land mass split down the middle of what today is the Atlantic Ocean, and that this happened before humans had evolved.
- <u>God's Word</u> says, in Genesis 7:11, that the earth broke up, and that Noah and his family spread throughout the world after the flood. It is very possible that some of the generations from Noah spread from Asia to Europe, and Africa, and also across, what was most likely, a short distance across the split, to what is now the Americas. Seas covered up vast amounts of land masses previously exposed, including cities now covered by water according to archeologists. Conventional science is quick to point out that ancient tablets from Nineveh (the famous Gilgamesh story), pre-date Moses. Further, that this version of a flood differs in many areas from the flood story recorded in Genesis. They therefore suggest that Moses rewrote the flood story from these older sources, meaning the Bible cannot be trusted. However, science has also discovered an even older tablet in Nippur dating from 2200 B.C., which supports the Genesis story in great detail—meaning that these stories which are closest to the time of the flood and Noah, actually record the most accurate history—they agree with Moses and the Bible. The Gilgamesh story is the re-make.
- <u>Science</u> says eventually humans evolved in Africa/Asia, and migrated to Alaska, and down the west side of the Americas.
- <u>God's Word</u> says, in Genesis 10:25, that the earth continued to split, and that people continued to scatter to all parts of the earth (Gen. 11:8). Ironically, God's Word actually fits the evidence better than the theory of science. The oldest finds in the Americas are not in Alaska, but on the Atlantic side, in Central and South America, across from Egypt, where the land split. Also, structures on both sides of the Atlantic are in pyramid form. Writings carved into a bowl in

Bolivia, at Tiahuanaco (the Fuente Magna Bowl), actually are written in Sumerian Cuneiform, dating to 3,000 B.C., a language associated with the ancient Babylonian area. Recent finds in Egyptian mummies show that they used large amounts of cocaine and tobacco, which both originated in the Americas, and mummification was common in both lands. Both Amazon and Egyptian art depict half humans and half animal beings, and both cultures link these to visions seen while in an altered state of consciousness from drug usage.

*   Science says, in the theory of plate tectonics, that the land masses moved slowly over millions of years, and only within the last 10-12,000 years have sea levels risen (as a result of the end of the great Ice Age), to cover vast areas of land masses previously exposed to life.

God's Word says, in Joshua 10:13-14 (1400 B.C.), and in Isaiah 38:8 (700 B.C.), that the earth stood still, and even rotated backwards. This was also reported by the Chinese in the book "*Worlds in Collision*" by Emanual Vibvkowski. The understanding is that there were massive shifts in the planet's surface (which is actually supported by the theory of earth-crust displacement which Albert Einstein offered). It is interesting to note that *all* of the world's calendars changed around the year of 700 B.C. from the 360/30-day earth/moon-cycle, by one seventieth, to the current 365.25/29.5 day cycle.

*   The major difference between the scientific theory and God's Word is *time*. In order for scientific theories to "seem" plausible, they must introduce massive amounts of time, and ages, but even with billions of years. The proof is still missing (see the Appendix).

Some scientists and researchers, such as Dr. Robert M. Scholch, of Yale, geologist/geophysicist, Robert Bauval, Graham Hancock, and John A.West, are pursuing a theory that the great achievements of the distant past, such as the Aztec calendar, with its advanced math and astronomy, the Mayan pyramids, the three great Egyptian pyramids of the Giza plateau, and the Sphinx, are all indicators of a great superior knowledge, which post-Stone Age people could not have possessed. They point out that recent evidence shows that these three great Egyptian pyramids, and the Sphinx (as well as Ankor Wat in Asia, and Tiahuanaco in Peru), all align perfectly with astronomical constellations, as they appeared in 10,500 B.C.

This early age was further confirmed by the weathering of the rock from which the Sphinx is constructed. Geology places the age of the Sphinx carving around 10,000 or more years ago. These findings were presented to the 1991 Geological society of America conference, and 275 geologists agreed with these findings. These findings were also debated in February 1992, at the American Association for the Advancement of Science, in Chicago.

Egyptologists counter that evolution is linear, and there could be no high intelligence in earlier periods. Their conference found that the science of Egyptology studies *monuments*, and these three Giza pyramids and the Sphinx, unlike the others in Egypt, have *no* markings of their builders, and *no* dates. Geologists study *geologic* evidence of wind and water *erosion*, which can be measured and dated. The Great Pyramid is attributed to Pharaoh Khufu due to a single cartouche which is displayed on a graffiti covered area. However, in 1837, British explorer Richard Howard Vyse states in his notes that there were *no* hieroglyphics in the great pyramid—just graffiti. Even so, until 2018, this single cartouche on the graffiti wall was considered enough evidence to assign the pyramids construction to Khufu. However, in 2018, a sample of the paint used on the cartouche was tested in Germany and has proven to be no older than 400 years, meaning the cartouche is also just graffiti.

Additionally, it turns out that the Sphinx, which has a body in the likeness of a lion, faces the horizon where, when the sun rises at the equinox, the constellation that was on the horizon in 10,500 B.C. was Leo the Lion.

Scientists all agree that the head of the Sphinx has been re-carved, and in the ancient temple of Esneh in Egypt the Sphinx has the head of a woman, which is pointing to the beginning order of the

Zodiac, or Virgo (a woman). Virgo, the constellation of the virgin, comes after Leo the Lion in the constellation order of the Zodiac.

This constellation alignment with the equinox changes every 2,160 years and, as an example, the constellation that was on the horizon during the time of Christ, 2,000 years ago, was Pisces (a fish). That is the reason Christians chose the fish as their symbol.

Egyptologists date these three great pyramids between 2575 B.C. and 2467 B.C., during the period of Taurus the Bull, with smaller pyramids being built before this time, and smaller pyramids continuing to be built after this time period.

It has been pointed out, however, that the three great pyramids are unique in more ways than just size. They, unlike all other Egyptian pyramids, have *no* markings, drawings, or pictographs. Their interior design and structure are unique. In fact, even to this day, no one has satisfactorily determined just how these three great pyramids were built. It seems they really were built long, long ago with a knowledge that has been lost.

The theory of these four researchers suggests the influence of a group of "mighty people,"—"mighty people who were of old,"—"people of renown," who passed on knowledge—but it has been lost since the ice age, which was triggered by a great flood and climate change (141, 143). Egyptian carvings depict a "staff of life" in many pictures, and this staff never touches the ground. Egyptian teaching for this is that the staff indicates that we are actually spiritual beings having an earth experience in mortal flesh bodies, but we will return to heaven (141).

Evidence I have pieced together from the disciplines of archeology, geology, and astronomy suggest that the three great pyramids of Giza were *not* built by Pharaohs Khufu, Khafre, and Menkaure, after other pyramids in Egypt had already been built. In fact, these three great pyramids were actually the very first pyramids built in Egypt. All the other pyramids were built after these three, and are of inferior quality. It is also possible that these were built before the great flood.

Geologist/geophysicist Robert Bauval has established the actual date for construction of the largest pyramid of Giza at 2450 B.C., and he established this date by its alignment with the constellation

Orion as it appeared in the year 2450 B.C. The layout of *all three* of the Giza pyramids actually align with Orion at a date of 10,500 B.C., which is the date Egypt places for what they call "the *First Time*," or the time of *creation*. At this date, Orion was at the lowest point, or beginning point in the precession cycle of earth, which is about 26,000 years.

The Hindu tradition is also of a cycle of about 13,000 years, which they call the cycle of progress, followed by a cycle of 13,000 years of decline (which we are entering now).

Egyptian tradition is that the first pyramids of the old kingdom (Aoser/Djoser), were built before the three Great Pyramids. Historian/archeologist David Rohl has provided evidence that the traditional dates for the pharaohs and their monuments are off by about 300 years, and the Aoser/Djoser pyramids were actually built around 2350 B.C. This means that the Great Pyramids of Giza were actually built *before* the other old kingdom pyramids.

The reason there are no pyramid structures for Khufu, Khafre, or Menkaure is because these structures were either too small, and have been destroyed over time, or because, as I theorize, these three pharaohs never even built any structures. During a 200-year period that included their reigns, Egypt and the entire world were experiencing a mini-Ice Age, as shown by evidence assembled by Egyptian archeologist, Fekri Hassan. Famine, death, and lack of labor were rampant. These Pharaohs *adopted* these three great Giza pyramids for themselves. This was also the period of time when Egyptologists think the Sphinx was constructed, or perhaps re-fur-bished, due to erosion. The head has been re-carved, to a smaller face of a pharaoh, probably from a face of a woman (as depicted in the Egyptian temple of Esneh dating to over 4,000 years ago). These three great pyramids are unique, and have no markings as do the other pyramids of Egypt.

Ironically, science, itself, is questioning today how post-Stone Age humans were able to construct the Egyptian pyramids, Sphinx, Ankor Wat in Asia, and Tiahuanaco in Peru, with their alignments to constellations dating back to 10,500 B.C. The ancient cultures of the Egyptians and the Maya (and possibly India), had knowledge of this 26,000 year precession cycle...how? (Genesis 6).

When the world was supposedly just emerging from the Stone Age, it's interesting to note that the Great Pyramid of Egypt had each of its sides constructed with a curvature inward, to signify the exact curvature of the earth. This is significant, because at this early date most everyone supposedly thought that the earth was flat.

Rene Noorbergen in *"Secrets of Lost Races: New Discoveries of Advanced Technology in Ancient Civilizations,"* states that in Peru, in Sacsayhuaman (Cuzco), huge stone blocks weighing up to 20,000 pounds were used in the construction (10—pgs. 196-197). This feat was not equaled in the modern world until the last century. This pre-Inca culture claimed that a giant from heaven called "Viracocha" had established these stone structures.

The Aymana Indians, around Lake Titicaca, tell of ancient beings from heaven who established Tiahuanaco, Puma Punku, and Ollantay Tambo (Urin Pacha), and founded their civilization (Gen. 6). Puma Punku, located at 12,800 feet in elevation, has smooth flat precision carved "H" interlocking stone blocks with recessed cuts, curves, and curved holes. These cannot be duplicated today except with very sophisticated mechanical cutting devices. No one knows how these stones, weighing up to 100 tons, were moved into place.

A short distance away from Puma Punku is Tiahuanaco, where stone walls have displayed on them carved heads of every race known to man, including a couple of unknown head shapes, and also a head shape with a large elongated brain cavity (similar to the giant skull found in Ur of Iraq). Both of these locations in Bolivia, tradition holds, were constructed by beings from the heavens with great power and knowledge. The creator god is named Viracocha, and is pictured with a beard and mustache, which is not part of the native culture, but is associated with the Sumerian culture on the other side of the world in the Mesopotamian area of Iraq dating to 3,000 B.C. A bowl discovered in the area of Tiahuanaco (Fuente Magna Bowl), has ancient Sumerian cuneiform writing carved in it.

In Peru, at Ollantay Tambo (Urin Pacha), stone structures are constructed with huge stones which are precision matched to fit, and somehow "fused" together without using cement. The cut surfaces of the stones are smooth, and include recessed notches, and appear to have saw and machine marks.

Also, science is questioning how later cultures, like the Mayan (whose knowledge of math and astronomy was seemingly far beyond human ability, without a higher power, or some outside higher intelligence), were able to develop their calendar and enormous stone buildings and pyramids, which have stones just as large as the pyramids of Egypt. Both Mayan/Aztec, and Egyptian histories refer to "giants" (Gen. 6:1-5). Prevalent in all these ancient cultures from all around the world are snake motifs in their art, and even in their crowns of gold worn by their kings (the gold crown to bring a shining highlight to the head—the source of knowledge--*the shining one*, or serpent, of Genesis 3:1-7).

It is interesting that up until the year 1517, when the Turks removed the white casing stones from the Great Pyramid to build their empire, the Great Pyramid in Egypt had a covering of polished white limestone blocks, each averaging thirty-five square feet in size. It is estimated these stones numbered 144,000. Ironically, this is the same number of Jews from the twelve tribes, to which Revelation 14:1 makes reference—another striking *imitation* of Christ's kingdom. Each of the three pyramids originally had a different color. The Great Pyramid was all white (some of the casing stones are still present at the top). The middle pyramid was all red, and the small pyramid was all black. The ancient Egyptians actually regarded the red pyramid as the primary pyramid because it represented balance between the other two—a balance the gods taught mankind to seek between the goddess and god, and between the female and male. In other words, don't elevate Jesus—there are many ways to heaven (John 14:6; Acts 4:12).

In Egypt, Karnak is a large temple complex dating its beginning to 3,000 B.C. It has engraved carvings in stone duplicated on the four sided obelisks which are carved *exactly* the same. These perfectly cut identical symbols could only have been duplicated like they are by mechanical means, which weren't available until today. Even the statues are all exact copies—perfectly replicated. They show machine tool markings comparable to modern mechanical tools. This knowledge supposedly came from the gods?

In Genesis, one will recall that God tells us of the "giants" and "mighty men," and warns us repeatedly not to worship these "sons of God," "the fallen ones," these "men of renown" (141, 143).

Ancient Egyptian texts refer to the *"First Time"* (Zep Tepi), the time of *creation*, as the era of the Neferu (Netheru– translated as human beings with god-like abilities). According to J.J. Champollion- Figeac in *Wisdom Literature*, Paris, 1888, the *Egyptian Book of the Dead* states that one of the "Company of the gods," Thoth, built the Great Pyramid according to a design which had descended from heaven. Ancient Sumerian texts speak of highly developed people who descended to the earth from the heavens, who developed into a people called the Nephilim. The Akkadians called them the Ilu, or the "High Ones," per Zecharia Sitchim, Sumerian language specialist.

Greek historian Herodotus wrote 2,400 years ago of the Great Pyramid's white casing stones being finely fitted together, polished, and engraved with signs and symbols. Jewish historian Josephus, 2,000 years ago also wrote of these, and noted the engravings recorded "a peculiar sort of wisdom." Eighth century Arab astronomer Abou Balkhi recorded in a scroll held at the Oxford University library, that the Great Pyramid was inscribed with the wonders of physics. The British museum holds a tenth century manuscript No. 9576, which records Arab historian Masoudi's testimony of the Great Pyramid as having carvings on the casing stones of celestial spheres and stars, their history, and progression. The Alexandrian library holds an eighth century book about Egypt's past called Camoos (Dictionary) of Firazabadi, which records that the Great Pyramid was built before the time of a great flood in ancient times. Herodotus records in his *Histories* that the Great Pyramid showed evidence of salt water calcification, as well as sea shells all around the area. This testimony was supported by Danish author Frederic Norden in the 1750's, who noted the great number of shells and oysters covering the plains around the pyramids (it should be noted that the Nile River has *no* shellfish, or salt water). The Alexandrian library holds a document written by Arab historian Ibn Abd Hokm that claims that some pyramids were built by a king, named Saurid Ibn Salhouk, more than 300 years before a great flood occurred, and that the Great Pyramid was already in existence at that time (141). Robert Bauval in *"Secret Chamber: The Quest for the Hall of Records"* notes that beneath the Sphinx, holes drilled struck red granite, instead of the natural limestone. Red granite is not native to the Giza plateau. Further, it is noted that drainage tubes extract water equal to three Olympic pools each day from beneath the Sphinx, indicating a great chamber is located under the Sphinx. The Egyptian authorities will not allow excavations, because any discovery of an ancient knowledge could destroy the Egyptian people's legacy.

All ancient civilizations tell of receiving great knowledge from beings from heaven (Gen. 6:1-5). In ancient Samaria (the oldest civilization), great knowledge sprang from nowhere, including written language, astronomy, chemistry, and mathematics. In the Sumerian myth, the god of water and wisdom (Gen. 1:1-5; Prov. 8), created man out of clay (Gen. 2:7-8), and the most powerful of gods, called Anu, was then superseded by a god called Enlil, the god of the air (Satan, Eph. 2:2; 2 Cor. 4:4). The oldest tablets found, dating to 2200 B.C., (CBM 13532), actually agree in great detail with the Genesis flood story of Noah. As mentioned already, in Bolivia, there was an ancient bowl (Fuente Magna Bowl), found at Tiahuanaco, which has ancient Sumerian cuneiform writing etched into it, and the god of that area (Viracocha), is pictured in statues at Tiahuanaco with a beard and mustache, similar to the men of Samaria on the other side of the world. These ancient "gods" had great knowledge and power, and ability to travel great distances, having come from the heavens. The clay cuneiform tablets found in the oldest Samaria site called Ur (Gen. 11:27ff), refer to a group of these heavenly gods called the Anunnaki, who possessed great power and knowledge (called the "Watchers" by the Egyptians). They are said to have had the ability to genetically alter humans—to cross breed them for the purpose of creating giants to perform hard work. In the 1927 excavation of Ur was discovered the remains of the queen, also known as the priestess (Queen Puabi). Her head is described as a "giant." Her skull was elongated, just as those found in Peru at Tiahuanaco.

Plato, in 360 B.C. wrote of the great city of Atlantis from before the flood of Noah. The Greek texts record that a being from heaven (called Poseidon), took a woman as his wife, had children by her, and founded Atlantis (Gen. 6:1-5).

Ancient Japan records beings from heaven called Dogu, who brought with them great knowledge, language, and building techniques. Jimmu (660 B.C.), the great one who established Japan, is said to have come from heaven.

The Hopi Indians, from Arizona, use Kachina dolls which are representations of beings from heaven. Their creator god Masau'u, came from the heavens with great knowledge and power. Their settlements at Black Mesa are arranged in a pattern which matches the constellation of Orion's belt, just like the great pyramids of Egypt, and the pyramids of Teotihuacan.

Teotihuacan, in Mexico, which dates to 3,114 B.C., is one of the largest cities in the ancient world. Its pyramids are laid out in the pattern of Orion's belt, just as the pyramids of Egypt, and the Hopi Indians of America at Black Mesa. The origin of the power to build the city with knowledge of the heavens is attributed to winged serpent gods.

The Sahara Desert holds ancient cave paintings showing beings from heaven.

In Iraq, two thousand year old batteries have been found around the ancient remains of Baghdad, which are capable of actually generating DC voltage. Babylonian tablets 2,700 years old, which were found here, record the movement of stars in great detail. This knowledge is only available to us today now that we have telescopes. Supposedly the gods from heaven brought civilization to this area long ago.

In India, the Hindu claim ancient prehistoric beings came from heaven to establish their land. Krishna (a primary god), came from heaven and founded the city of Dwaraka. Sangam legends in India also tell of beings from heaven with great knowledge and power. The "Divali" (Festival of Light), in India celebrates King Rama (5,000 B.C.), bringing with him power and knowledge from heaven. Rama is said to have designed the ancient city of Vijayanagara to reflect the cosmic universe. The Lord of Creation, Mamuni Mayan, is said to have lived in this city after arriving from the heavens.

Stonehenge, in England, has concentric circles which relate accurately to the path of the planets circling the sun. In our history, we know that people thought that the earth (not the sun) was at the center of the solar system. But, the builders of Stonehenge knew the truth about our solar system, and these stones are also aligned to define the positions of the sun and moon during the equinoxes.

Where did this knowledge and power to move these stones and align them come from? King Woden (Oden — god of wind), is credited with coming from heaven with great powers to England.

Around Italy, at Malta, the ancient stone structures date to a thousand years older than the Egyptian pyramids, and the construction techniques are equal to technologies available only today. Again, credit for knowledge and power is given to gods from the heavens.

The Minoan people were leaders during the bronze age, and shipwrecks from that time show copper ore being transported. Geologist Scott Wolter, in 2014, is developing evidence which shows that the Minoan people were mining their copper from the Great Lakes region of the United States thousands of years ago. The mineral chemical signature of the copper in America does match the copper from the Minoan shipwrecks. It has long been known that a billion tons of copper which were mined from the Great Lakes region cannot be accounted for, unless, the copper was used to develop the bronze age needs.

In Ethiopia, at a large site called Lalibela, eleven temples have been carved into solid rock. These buildings are not visible to a person standing on the ground at a distance. These multistory buildings are carved down into the earth — carved down into the stone from the roof upstairs to the lower floors downstairs. The buildings, both outside, as well as rooms inside, are all carved from a single stone rock. Tradition is that angels helped build these, and when the Ark of the Covenant, in the temple of Solomon, disappeared hundreds of years before Jesus Christ, that it was transported to this site in Ethiopia. One of the temples does have an alter the exact dimensions of the Ark of the Covenant. Today, the Ethiopians claim to have the Ark of the Covenant in an underground chamber at a temple in Aksum.

In Lebanon, at the site known today as Heliopolis (so named by the Greeks), is an even more ancient stone building site called Baalbek, upon which Heliopolis was built. Baalbek (a reference to the sun god of Babylon), is the site of huge stones erected possibly even before the great pyramids of Egypt. These stones weigh up to 1,200 tons, and they are perfectly matched together. The Sumerians wrote over 5,000 years ago how the gods from heaven came to this place.

The Greek legends record that Zeus (the sun god), and Apollo (the son of Zeus), were beings from the heavens with great power and knowledge (Gen. 6:1-5). The story is that out of Zeus came Hera (like Eve from Adam—Gen. 2:22). Hera's name was changed to Athena after a great flood (Gen. 6:17), and she supposedly received her great powers and authority from the serpent—the source of knowledge in the Greek understanding (Gen. 3:4-6).

In Armenia, Carahunge is an 8,000 year old stone circle (older than Stonehenge), where the stones are aligned to the constellation Cygnus (the swan, or the vulture). Many cultures have myths about the power of Cygnus, and ancient gods from heaven.

In Egypt, the Book of the Dead records that the Egyptian people fled from the "Land of the Watchers" (called the Anunnaki in Samaria). These "Watchers" supposedly came from heaven and were originally known as the Nibiru. The Nibiru ruled and judged man. The Bible records these names as the Anakim and the Nephilim, and they are references to beings from heaven, as well as the children born from them to human women (Gen. 6:1-12). The Dead Sea Scrolls reveal that about 200 of these fallen angels (Watchers) came to earth (Jude 6), 42 of which served Osiris according to the Egyptian *Book of the Dead*. The fear of these Watchers elevated Isis (the sister/wife of Osiris), as she supposedly could protect humans because of her power granted from the serpent to overpower these Watchers (fallen angels). Magic pagan practices through Isis came out of this fear of these fallen angels/ Watchers (145). Note that Daniel 4 mentions "Watchers" as angels, and the Hebrew word denotes good and evil watchers.

In their book *"Discovery of Genesis,"* C.H. Kang, and Dr. Ethel R. Nelson report on prehistoric Chinese idiographic pictures used in ancient Chinese writings depicting the creation of man in the Garden of Eden, the temptation and fall, Noah's flood with eight people surviving, and the Tower of Babel—all biblical. The Chinese myths record their civilization began with a great being from heaven called the Sun of Heaven, who brought with him powers and knowledge. Ava Ford M.D. reports that ancient Chinese states that all people on earth descend from Nu-wa (Noah) Ancient Chinese worshiped what was called "One true God." These ancient Chinese language symbols are found in cuneiform on clay tablets dating back to 2250 B.C.—the approximate date of the flood. It is interesting that both the Olmec of Meso America, and the ancient Chinese share much in their ancient languages...indicating a common source sometime in the past. Ancient Chinese scholar Han Ping Chen when visiting Olmec sites and exhibits remarked *"I can easily read this—these are Chinese characters."* Furthermore, the Aztec board game of Patolli uses similar rules to the Chinese game of Parcheesi. It is common practice in both the Olmec culture and the Chinese Shang culture to place a jade bead into the mouth of a deceased person. The Olmec and Shang existed at about the same time in history.

In the Bible, Paul writes of the third heaven—another dimension (2 Cor. 12:2). Jesus told us that His kingdom was not of this world—(it was of another dimension (John 18:36).

Genesis 6 records that angels from heaven took women and had strange children from them—giants of great power and knowledge. This was Satan's plan to destroy and genetically alter the bloodline of humans, so that the Savior (Jesus), could not be born (Gen 3:14-15). God saved Noah, who had a pure *bloodline* (Gen. 6:8-9—the Hebrew is "bloodline"), and God destroyed the evil up to that time, with the flood.

We are told in the Bible that our battle is not really against flesh and blood, but against forces outside our dimension—spirit forces (Eph. 6:12).

From the Bible itself, to all the pagan myths recorded around the world—all this recorded information tells us that what is recorded in the Bible, about fallen angels and evil causing God to bring a flood, is supported by historical evidence. The Bible is true, and so is the reality of Satan's influence in our lives (Eph. 2:2; 2 Cor. 4:4). Yet, millions of people, who are aware of the Bible, willingly choose to wander the planet and not study God's Word. These people are willingly ignorant (2 Pet. 3:1-7).

Science and history is pointing in the same direction that Moses wrote about thousands of years ago, in Genesis 6. These "mighty men" were worshiped as gods, by the humans God had birthed into the earth, and God had to destroy these early civilizations, including even the babies, with the flood. The knowledge and power of these "mighty men" was lost to future generations of humans. Even today, we are still mystified by these past civilizations of "intelligence."

In Job 8:9, and Ecclesiastes 9:11, we are told there was more knowledge in the past, and there is nothing new now.

Egyptologists, the scientists who study the pyramids, are puzzled as to why pyramids, supposedly built *before* the three Great Pyramids of Giza, are just like the pyramids supposedly built *after* the three Great Pyramids. They are *all* falling apart, except the three. Only the three Great Pyramids are surviving well. These three Great Pyramids are unique, different from all the other one hundred or so pyramids in Egypt.

Daniel 12:4 says that in the end times knowledge will increase. New evidence, in the last couple of years, now available to geologists and cultural scientists, points out that it is very likely that these three Great Pyramids, which are unique and unlike any other of the Egyptian pyramids (even if built only 4,500 years ago), were built to express knowledge of astronomy dating to 12,500 years ago, including the cycle of precession. Knowledge available only to a "mighty" people. Knowledge which was immediately lost after the age of the old kingdom in Egypt, as all other newer pyramids are of poorer construction and quality.

Christopher Dunn in *"The Giza Power Plant: Technologies of Ancient Egypt,"* states that there are no markings of the builders in these three great pyramids. The base of the great pyramid is curved inward, to match the earth circumference. The casing stones weigh between 16 and 20 tons each, and are cut to joint tolerances of .020 inches. The cement used to connect them together is actually stronger than the marble stone itself. The composition of the cement is still a mystery to science today (101—pg. 103). Even today, modern rock quarries cannot match the precision tolerances achieved by the Egyptians for the blocks of the pyramids. There are thousands of blocks, weighing 15 tons each, and about 100, weighing 70 tons each, in the great pyramid. Science has estimated that it would require that 31 stone blocks be set in place every hour, for 10 hours a day, for 365 days a year for 20 years to complete the great pyramid (101—pg. 128-133).

Science discovered that the unique character of the Egyptian Coffins at Saqqara, show saw markings that were made to hollow out the giant coffins. These saw markings do not match hand sawing, but match *modern-day* machine loop-wire sawing techniques. Sir W. M. Flinders Petrie, in *"The Pyramids and Temples of Gizeh,"* states that these giant coffins, which were to house the remains of the giant Apis bulls, weigh 65 tons each, are 13 feet long, 7.5 feet wide, and 11 feet tall. In the 1850's, 60 of them were discovered buried in this tomb. Their sides are polished so fine, that even today's technology, cannot match the tolerances the Egyptians achieved (101—pg. 124-125). Also, the carving out of vases and core drillings, all show evidence of mechanical processes not known until modern times. These markings of mechanical tools are even found in the hardest of stone, and today, we still do not know how the Egyptians did it (101—pg. 114-123).

The Egyptians used iron as well as copper. Iron was used in some limestone joints to link them (101—pg. 109). D. T. Bayard, in *"Early Thai Bronze"* in *Science*, June 1972, states that Ancient Egypt and Samaria used both brass and iron metallurgy. Bronze-age miners produced 22 pound copper ingots, which were ninety-seven percent pure (101—pg. 45). Samaria (the oldest civilization), records that their great knowledge, including written language, astronomy, chemistry, and math, sprang from beings who came from heaven (Gen. 6). In China, the Jin Dynasty (which existed from 265 to 420 A.D.), isolated aluminum from ore 1,500 years before today's scientists "rediscovered" how to do it (101—pg. 8-9). The Chinese civilization has many links to Noah and the biblical stories in Genesis. Chinese ideographic pictures used in ancient Chinese writings depict the creation of man, the Garden of Creation, the temptation and fall, Noah's flood with eight people surviving, and the tower of Babel (145).

The Sphinx has been shown by geologists to be about 10,000 years old, based upon water erosion evidence, even though conventional Egyptologists, with no direct evidence of age, continue to disagree. Additionally, the Sphinx faces east, to the horizon, where, when the sun rises on the equinox, the constellation which would have been in the heavens in the year 10,500 B.C., would have been Leo, the Lion—the form of the Sphinx, the constellation which follows Virgo, the virgin. The ancient temple of Esneh, in Egypt, shows the head of the Sphinx as a woman's head pointing to Virgo, and the body of a lion facing toward Leo, in the Zodiac. All science agrees the head of the Sphinx has been re-carved to the image of a Pharaoh. Perhaps, it used to be the head of a woman.

All this is evidence that the age of the Sphinx, the Giza Pyramids, Ankor Wat, and Tiwanaku are pointing to that period of time around 10,000 to 12,000 years ago, a date known by Egyptologists as *"The First Time."*

At this point it would be proper to clarify how the age of structures relates to the dates Bible scholars place for the beginning of the generations of Adam and Eve.

The date traced back to the beginning of Genesis is between 6,000 and 13,000 years ago, according to Bible scholars. This is the period of the "mighty men," the "sons of God," who took to themselves daughters of men (Gen. 6:1-5).

If one's view of the generations of Adam and Eve goes back 13,000 years, there is no problem understanding that the Sphinx and other structures could be that old.

But, if the pyramids, the Sphinx, and other structures such as Ankor-Wat in Asia, and Tiahuanaco in Peru, currently under study, are determined to be aligned with constellations dating to 12,500 years, how does this affect God's Word for those who hold to the 6,000 years of generations from Adam and Eve?

Ironically, the message is basically the same. Whether these structures were actually built by the mighty men 12,000 years ago, and aligned to stars existing in the heavens at that time, or whether these mighty men built these structures about 4,500 years ago to mark **A**) some past date of Satan's rebellion against God in the former earth age, or **B**) perhaps, as a reference to the "*First Time*" recorded by the ancient Egyptians, which would demonstrate "knowledge" of earth's 26,000 year tilt cycle, called precession (every 72 years equals one degree of movement in the sky), the results are the same. These structures were built long ago, causing many to worship false gods, the rebelling, or fallen angels, their earthly power and "knowledge", and causing earthly women to give themselves to them (Gen. 6:2-4). The Hindu tradition also refers to a cycle of 13,000 years of progress (which has just ended), followed by 13,000 years of decline.

One will note that even though the Bible refers to Egypt hundreds of times, God never mentions the greatest of all structures in the world, the pyramids and the Sphinx. Why is God's word silent about these greatest of all structures on earth?

The constellations, like Leo the Lion, and Taurus the Bull, move through the heavens very slowly. Every 2,160 years a new constellation appears on the horizon as the sun rises on the equinox. For example, when Jesus was on earth, the constellation then was Pisces the Fish. This is why the early Christians chose the fish as their symbol, not to worship the stars, but as a time reference, a calendar, if you will. The constellations were used, not only for worship at the time of Christ, but also as a celestial calendar, a point of reference in time. The Zodiac was originally God's plan of salvation (100).

In the oldest book in the Bible, Job 38:32 (2150 B.C.), there is the reference to the Mazzaroth (the Zodiac), which in Hebrew and Sanskrit means "The Way," or "The Path." In all the ancient nations the *same* 12 constellations in the *same* order with the *same* pictures are referenced as far back in antiquity as one can go. It has been pointed out by scholars, and historians like Josephus, that this common source for the Zodiac worldwide has been attributed to God's plan of salvation, which was given to Adam and Eve to pass onto all the generations, so that all would be called to salvation (142, 143).

While the story of the Zodiac goes from Virgo to Leo, as indicated by the sphinx figure in the temple of Esneh, in Egypt, the twelve constellations actually appear on the equinox horizon, going in the opposite order—from Leo to Virgo. Thus, there are two paths leading from beginning to end. When and where they cross is interesting.

God has actually created for us three views of His Plan.

A) The horizon sequence of constellations: God created the universe and set the earth and stars in motion, and we observe the constellations on the horizon, beginning in order from **Leo** to **Taurus,** to Pisces to **Aquarius,** to **Scorpio** to Virgo. These constellations actually match the sequence in God's plan told in the Zodiac (see "B" next), only the order, as seen on the horizon, is reversed from the way God tells the story in the Zodiac.

B) God's plan sequence of the Zodiac: God uses the stars to tell the story of good and evil, God and Satan, and man and salvation. God sets the sequence of the story in the Zodiac beginning in order, from Virgo to **Scorpio,** to **Aquarius** to Pisces, to **Taurus** to **Leo.** The constellations actually match the Horizon sequence, only God's order of the story is in reverse to "man's view" of the Horizon sequence.

C) God's sequence for Israel: God establishes the twelve tribes of Israel, and tied each to a constellation name and gives Moses instructions for the tribes to follow a given order, under their tribal standards (Num. 2-3. These same four main orders are also seen by Ezekiel [Ezek. 10], and John [Rev. 4], but are not mentioned as being in any particular order). The order given by God in Numbers, does not match the order God gave in either the Horizon sequence or God's Zodiac sequence. The order here begins with **Leo** and goes then to **Aquarius** and Pisces, then to **Taurus**, and finally to **Scorpio.** God, being in control, is calling our attention to: 1) The image formed by the tribes in the desert (a cross), and 2) The constellations of Gemini and Taurus, and the story God tells in conjunction with the meeting in 2012 of the constellations of Pisces and Aquarius.

It was during the time of Leo 12,500 years ago, that Osiris (Orion) was at its low point in Earth's precession cycle. The Egyptians called this low point *"The First Time,"* and it seems the Great Pyramids are aligned to commemorate this date of 10,500 B.C. The high point for Osiris (Orion) occurred in 2012 when Pisces and Aquarius met on the horizon during the precession cycle.

Here is the way God's plan (God's story) is told in each of the three ways God has given it to man:

1) The **Horizon sequence** (man's view), matches Jesus coming to us 2,000 years ago, at the beginning of the Pisces constellation (fish—Christians), and His salvation being available to man during all these years. Beginning in 2012, Aquarius became the center of attention (man--mankind has now elevated himself above God).

2) **God's Plan sequence of the Zodiac** gives us a picture of God offering forgiveness and salvation (Capricorn), and then 2,000 years ago, man rejected Christ (Aquarius), and we now are entering the period when Christ will return (Pisces).

3) **The Twelve Tribe sequence** in the desert, places Gemini and Taurus in a sequence parallel with Pisces and Aquarius in 2012. The names given to the stars of these constellations (before recorded time), give us a picture of the twin images of Jesus in Gemini, as the Sufferer, and as the Ruler, meeting Taurus, which is the twin image of the ox (judgment) in the same image with a lamb (Savior)—a picture of the end times.

All three of these met in the year of 2012, and 2012 also began the reversal in the precession cycle of the *"First Time,"* in Egyptian chronology. Is this the Last Time? The Mayan Calendar recorded that 2012 will be the end of a cycle, and the calendar ends. Islam holds to a prophecy that we entered the end times period in 1956, in the midst of the dates of 1948, when Israel was restored to the land, and 1967 when Jerusalem was restored to Israel. Islam's prophecy is that Jesus will return and give power to Islam sometime before 2076, which is their prophecy's last possible date for the end to occur. God tells us we will not know the day or the hour of His return, but God also warns us to be watchful and prepared.

Satan is the great imitator. Is it possible that Satan will use this period of time for the beast of Revelation 13 to arrive – the "savior" (small "s") of the "world" (this world's ways)? Time will tell. God tells us no one knows the date, but God Himself.

Now that we have arrived at the change of constellations since 2012, let's note some of the major stars' names in Aquarius: Scheat, Markab, Deneb, and Azel, all meaning: *"The Judge returns from afar quickly,"* and in Pisces, the stars of Al Deramin and Al Phirk, meaning: *"The redeemer is coming quickly."* In Egyptian, Pisces means *"fishes that belong to the one who is coming."*

It is obvious to Christians that God would not want anyone worshiping stars, moons, or constellations. God created the heavens— only humans choose to make idols out of them. But, God does use our customs and traditions to suit His purpose, even if they are not His perfect will.

For example, the Magi from Babylon were used by God to announce to the world the great event that was about to take place in Bethlehem. David Huges, astronomer from Sheffield University, in England, has studied the cuneiform tablets from Babylon and traced the time period of the birth of Christ.

The Israelite people did not understand exactly *when* the Savior was to come, but they knew from the prophets, *where* He was to be born. It was to be in Bethlehem (Matt. 2:4-8; Micah 5:2).

The Magi, by studying astronomy, decided a great event was about to happen to the Israelite people, but did not know *where* (Matt. 2:2). The Magi saw in the heavens several rare events, including Jupiter and Saturn going through a triple conjunction (over a period of several months), and Jupiter and Regulus also going through triple conjunctions. These conjunctions appeared as bright stars, and because this activity was occurring in the constellation of Pisces (the Babylonian sign for the Israelite peoples), they decided this great event was for the Israelite people (see *The Birth of Christ* section next).

It would seem God chose this timing as the way of announcing to the world the birth of Christ. The Babylonians were well-known, and recognized as a worldly center of knowledge and power at this time.

Satan's use of astrology today is another example of his imitating God. Many in the world today believe, falsely, that there is some kind of "power" in the study of the heavens. Satan is continually deceiving people with falsehoods and imitations (2 Cor. 11:13-15; Rev. 12:7-9, 13:11).

If the pyramids are traced in age to the same time period of Genesis, where God tells us of "mighty men" and "sons of God," why would these fallen angels (some 6,000 to 12,000 years ago), pick the shape of a pyramid for their greatest monuments? Is this possibly one of the greatest imitations of all? Were pyramids picked because, as we know from the Bible, Satan was actually trying to imitate God and Christ's eternal power?

If Satan wanted to imitate God, what better way than a pyramid, (which is arguably the shape of the "New Jerusalem" described in Revelation 21:16-17)?

One cannot say for sure whether Revelation 21:16-17 refers to a cube or a pyramid. It seems obvious that the "mighty ones" (Gen. 6:1-5), who built the pyramids, were trying to build a place of the gods, and it would appear Satan thinks God's plan calls for a pyramid. Satan is only an imitator, and is not perfect, despite his power. God's "New Jerusalem," of course, will be perfect and everlasting. The pyramids of Egypt and Central America are, at best, only imitations, built by "mighty men," not by God.

Again, we are also reminded of recent evidence which shows that the pyramids built *after* these great pyramids of old, are all of very poor construction. Is this because the "knowledge" was lost? The other one hundred or so pyramids in Egypt are only imitations of these three great pyramids, built long ago. And, the three Great Pyramids, it would seem, are themselves, only imitations of God's plan. Perhaps the "great high mountain" of Revelation 21:10, is a reference to the new Jerusalem pyramid.

The Mayan pyramids of Teotihuacan also are unique. There are three main pyramids there also, and they are also placed in a similar pattern to the three great Egyptian pyramids. Science has not been able to date these pyramids of the Maya, but earthquake evidence has placed them *older* than the Egyptian pyramids. The history of the Mayans (passed down to the Aztecs), also indicates they were built by "giants," long *before* the time of the Maya.

Another study of these Mayan pyramids by Hugh Harleston Jr., an American engineer, in a presentation to the International Congress of Americanists, in 1974, links the overall layout pattern of the entire area to a scale model of the solar system, *including* the outer planets, which were not known of until the eighteenth and nineteenth centuries — not to mention that modern scientists (before Galileo), thought the earth was at the center.

The concentric circles of Stonehenge in England, also are a scale representation of the planets circling the sun — again, when modern scientists (before Galileo), thought the earth was at the center.

In Turkey, at a site called Gobekli Tepe (estimated to be the oldest site in the world dating to 10,000 years ago), there are many stone circles with columns nineteen feet tall with animals not native to Turkey carved into the stones. Obviously these people had great knowledge, but from where?

Ancient people in all parts of the world possessed knowledge which we have only recently "rediscovered." The Jin Dynasty in China shows evidence of being able to isolate aluminum from ore. Modern science only recently was able to do this (101 — pg. 8-9).

The use of optics are shown by ancient man, in a book by Robert Temple, *"The Crystal Sun: Rediscovering a Lost Technology of the Ancient World."* The rings of Saturn are depicted in drawings from ancient times, and without optics to aid the eye, one cannot see these rings, even today. Also, in this book, he discussed that in ancient Egypt they had the ability to do complex grinding, polishing, and hollowing, which, even today, is difficult to duplicate. The Egyptians had both convex and concave lenses, and could carve so small, that today, a magnifying glass is needed to read the carvings. Also in Peru, the ancient Nazca could write so small, that today, just like in Egypt, a microscope is needed to read the writings (101—pg. 82-87).

Rising sea waters covered vast areas of land 4,000-5,000 years ago. The exposed land masses used to be closer and more accessible to sea travel than today. There are many evidences of contact from Japan, Europe, and Africa to the Americas, thousands of years ago. The prevailing currents from the straits of Gibraltar actually go to Brazil. Scientific studies done early in 2002, suggest that Carel, an ancient site in Peru, dates to 2600 B.C., which would make it the oldest major civilized site in the world, even older by a hundred years than the Egyptian sites.

In the Amazon areas of South America, science has discovered hundreds of miles of canals dating to the age of the first dynasty of Egypt. These canals linked raised grounds with raised pyramids, and the purpose of the raised grounds was to provide food. The black soils found in this Amazon area, to this day, are more productive than even the fertilized soils of the rest of the world. According to Dr. Clark Erickson, of the University of Penn., Professor William Balee of Tulane University, Professor William Woods of South Ill. Univ., and Dr. Michael Heckenberger of the University of Florida, these ancient people of the Amazon areas are related to the Europeans in language sources, and tribal rites, and they had better agriculture techniques than we possess today. Tiahuanaco, at 12,000 feet in altitude, produced seven times the average yield of land using modern techniques today.

In South America, the oldest civilization, located on the eastern part of the continent, are the Olmec, and their statues resemble Black Africans. In Brazil, the oldest skull discovered is a Black African skull. In Peru, in Tiahuanaco (in the sunken garden), are carved faces depicting every racial type known (101—pg. 191).

Ancient Chinese scholar, Han Ping Chen, has identified ancient Chinese characters (writings from the Shang Dynasty—1200 B.C.), on an Olmec sculpture of a head (also 1200 B.C.—the large Olmec heads are famous in Central and South America). Other ancient links between Meso-America, and ancient China include: 1) The ancient Aztec board game of "Patolli," which is very similar to

Parcheesi; 2) The focus of both China and Meso-America on the tiger, the jaguar, and dragon like creatures; and 3) The use of Jade beads in the mouth of a deceased person, which both the Shang Dynasty of China (1200 B.C.), and the Olmec of Meso-America (1200 B.C.), used. Another interesting connection between the Maya of South and Central America, and East Asians, is reported by S.G. Morley in his book: *"The Ancient Maya"* Stanford University Press). Both have the physical characteristics of the epicanthic eye fold (a fold at the inner corner of the eye), and also, the unique physical characteristic of what is known as the "Mongolian Spot" (a bluish spot at the base of the spine, which is present at birth, and usually disappears by age ten). There is also the evidence of shared knowledge of construction of ziggurats by the Aztecs and Chinese, as well as the use of cylindrical seals. All these connections suggest a connection between these two continents around 4,200 years ago (about the time of Noah's flood—141).

Charles Hapgood in *"Maps of the Ancient Sea Kings,"* states that ancient maps show features we can today only see by using modern instruments (101—pg. 12, 58-63).

Conventional science, it seems, will accept theories of slow plate tectonics, magnetic core reversals within the earth, and crustal displacement on Mars, but have been reluctant to agree with Albert Einstein concerning catastrophic shifts of the Earth's crust, or other "unconventional" evidence, showing that the people of the earth had a common source recently in history.

BIRTH OF CHRIST: *WHEN?*

See *Target Truth Ministries*.com
for News & Updates

T here are four primary dates identified by scholars for the date
of Christ's birth:6 B.C., 4B.C., 3 B.C., 2 B.C.

There are clues in scripture we can analyze.

- The timing of the birth and ministry of John the Baptist
  (Luke 1:5-37, 3:1-3).

- Luke 3:1: John began his ministry in the fifteenth year of
  Tiberius Caesar, which began in August 19, 14 A.D. So the
  fifteenth year was August of 28 A.D., to August of 29 A.D.
  John would have been at least thirty (Luke 3:23), pointing
  to 2 B.C. as the birth date of John, with the birth of Jesus to
  follow. Some say the year for the birth of John the Baptist
  may have been earlier (by one year), in 3 B.C.

- Luke 1:8-38: John was born six months before Jesus.

- Luke 1:5: Zacharias, the father of John the Baptist, served
  in the eighth rotation of duty at the temple (Abijah, or Abia),
  which, if in 4 B.C., would have been the week of May
  19-26, and if in 3 B.C. would have been the week of July
  6-13. The eighth rotation occurred twice in a year, however,

the winter dates would have resulted in a winter birth for Jesus (9 months, plus 6 months)...not a time for shepherds to be in the fields, so these winter rotation dates are not discussed here. In Luke, we read that he couldn't finish his rotation, and went back to Elizabeth his wife, and she conceived John. Two hundred and eighty days after these two possible dates of 4 or 3 B.C., would result in a birth date for John of February/March of 3 B.C., or March/April of 2 B.C. Again, Jesus birthdate could be either 3B.C., or 2 B.C.

- The timing of the birth and ministry of Jesus—six months after John the Baptist (Luke 1:36, 2:1-40, 3:23; Matt. 1:20-23, 2:1-23). Six months later for the birth of Jesus would be on the Feast of Trumpets, September 11th of 3 B.C., or on the *Feast of Trumpets (September 29th of 2 B.C.)*.

- The Shepherds—the latest the shepherds would keep their flocks in the fields in Palestine would be October.

- There are also clues in the writings of early historians relating to the Scriptures:

Tertullian: Wrote of Herod's death on January 14, 1 B.C.

Josephus: Wrote of Herod's death in 1 B.C. after the eclipse of the moon (mistakenly copied as 4 B.C. in documents copied after 1552 A.D.--see remarks later).

Astronomy: Eclipses of the moon occurred in March 23, 5 B.C., September 15, 5 B.C., March 13, 4 B.C., and January 10, 1 B.C.

Tertullian: Wrote that Augustus began to rule 41 years before the birth of Jesus, and Augustus died 28 years after the birth of Jesus, or **2 B.C.**

Irenaeus: Wrote that Augustus began to rule in the autumn of 43 B.C. and Jesus was born in the 41st year of his rule, or **2 B.C.** (possibly 3 B.C., depending upon month Augustus rule began.

Tertullian: Wrote that Jesus was born 28 years after the death of Cleopatra, who died in 30 B.C. **(2 B.C.)**.

Eusebius: Wrote that Augustus began to rule in the autumn of 43 B.C. and Jesus was born in the 42nd year of his rule, and born the 28th year after the death of Cleopatra in 30 B.C. The 42nd year ran from autumn of 2 B.C. to autumn of 1 B.C. and the 28th year ran from autumn of 3 B.C. to autumn of 2 B.C. So, the *autumn of 2 B.C.* is the period of Christ's birth.

Historians: Agree that the 15th year of Tiberius's rule is from August of 28 A.D. to August of 29 A.D. Therefore, John the Baptist would begin his ministry during this period, and if 30 years old, the traditional age for a Rabbi (see Luke 3:23), he would be born sometime in 3 to 2 B.C., and Luke 1:5 (discussion above), points to spring 2 B.C. Spring and summer represent preferable months to perform baptisms, compared to winter.

John 2:19-20:

1) Jesus first early act--age 30, just after His baptism.
2) Herod began Temple construction in 19 B.C.
3) 46 years after construction is 27 A.D., and Jesus is 30+, which would make Jesus birth as early as 3 B.C., but...it states 46 years *in building* (*not since*--could be 47 or 48, which would equal 2 B.C., or 1 B.C.

THE CENSUS: There was a requirement by Augustus to either swear allegiance to the emperor, or pay a tax, in preparation for the special Roman Jubilee Year of February of 2 B.C. The registration could have begun in 3 B.C. and taken at least a year to cover the entire Roman Empire, and should have been concluded in 2 B.C. sometime. Josephus wrote that an oath of allegiance was demanded by Augustus about 12 to 15 months before the death of Herod, so the registration could have been begun as early as February of 3 B.C. (12 months before the Jubilee Year of February of 2 B.C.), and lasted as late as the death of Herod in January of 1 B.C., considering that Rome allowed at least one year for a registration to be completed.

- The Magi: Something caused the magi to: **1)** Begin a journey to Jerusalem, **2)** Follow events on their journey which would have taken two to four months travel time, and **3)** View a specific event as significant, when the star seemed to stop (Matt. 2:9). The magi were interpreters of dreams, and astrologers, who knew of the prophecies of Daniel, from Daniel's time in Babylon, during the captivity (Dan. 5). The prophecies (Dan. 9), spoke of the Messiah coming sometime during this period of time of the first century, and the magi were looking for it to be fulfilled. They looked for *signs* (Gen. 1:14 – God's story originally told in the Zodiac (142, 143).

- **The Magi Understanding was:**
  Aries = Judea, **Pisces** = Hebrews, **Virgo** = virgin, **Leo** = Judah, **Sun** = supreme father, **Moon** = supreme mother, **Regulus** = the king star in Leo, **Venus** = the brightest planet - the goddess (Ishtar), **Jupiter** = 2nd brightest planet – the king, **Saturn** = the protector of the Jewish people, **Mercury** = messenger of the gods.

In 7 B.C.: The magi witnessed a triple conjunction of Jupiter and Saturn in Pisces. These occurred in May, September, and December of 7 B.C. This is a very rare occurrence, meaning a king (Jupiter), was to be born to the Hebrew people (Pieces), to bring protection (Saturn).

In 6 B.C.: In February, three planets overlapped each other in Pisces (Jupiter, Mars, and Saturn), another very rare occurrence.

<u>In 6 B.C.</u>: In April, there was a conjunction between Jupiter and the Moon, in Aries. Coins of 6 B.C. show Aries, the lamb, looking at a star.

<u>In 4 B.C.</u>: This is a date referred to by many as the correct date, and it relates primarily to the writings of Josephus, which were copied *after* 1552 A.D., which linked 4 B.C. to the date for the birth of Jesus. Prior to 1552 A.D., the older manuscripts read 1 B.C. Coins were discovered which were dated to the period of 4 B.C., which were coined to show the successors of Herod (Archelaus, Antipas, and Philip). Therefore, it was assumed that the correct date was 4 B.C. However, evidence now shows that it was very common practice for rulers to date the reign of a new king to some date *before* his predecessor's death, so as to ensure his right to the title, and the treasury.

<u>August 12, 3 B.C.</u>: Jupiter (king planet), and Venus overlap (the first of a triple conjunction)--2nd-July 17 2 BC--3rd--Oct. 12 2 BC.

<u>September 11, 3 B.C.</u>: Jupiter and Regulus (king star in Leo constellation), overlapped in Leo, and the Sun is located in Virgo (the sun is in Virgo for 20 days each year). See Revelation 12 discussion at the end of this section (142). Some say this is the birth date, but it could be the one year *announcement* of Jesus' birth.

<u>February 17, 2 B.C.</u>: Jupiter and Regulus overlap for the 2nd time, and they overlap with the Moon also.

<u>May 8-9, 2 B.C.</u>: Jupiter and Regulus overlap for the 3rd time, and again they also overlap with the Moon.

<u>June 17, 2 B.C.</u>: A very rare occurrence in Leo, along with the Sun and Moon, the two brightest planets of Venus and Jupiter all overlap. This would result in the brightest "*star*" ever seen, and in the near-east this only occurred this one time in over 2,000 years.

<u>August 27, 2 B.C.</u>: Jupiter while moving westward, overlaps with Mars and Venus and Mercury, all in Leo.

<u>September 29, 2 B.C.</u>: Sun and moon in Virgo. See Rev. 12 discussion at the end of this section (142). The magi set off on their journey to seek this great king to be born to the Hebrew people... based upon these signs.

<u>December 25, 2 B.C.</u>: Jupiter in Virgo appeared to stop for six days (due to retrogression of the planet – a normal occurrence). From a vantage point in Jerusalem (where the Magi were), Jupiter would have appeared stopped over Bethlehem. Of course, when the Magi stopped in Jerusalem to inquire about a king being born, the child had already been born (Matt. 2:11 – a child, not a baby, and He was in the house, not a manger). This would be months *after* the birth of Jesus.

<u>SEQUENCE</u>:

<u>John the Baptist born</u> – March/April of 2 B.C. – This represents the most likely sequence to fit all the available evidence.

Jesus born Sept. 29 of 2 B.C.

Jesus dedicated 40 days later	November, 2 B.C.
Magi visit Jerusalem	December 25, 2 B.C.
Jesus taken to Egypt	January 1 B.C.
Herod ordered babies killed	January 1 B.C.
Eclipse of the Moon	January 10, 1 B.C.
Herod dies	January 14, 1 B.C.
Jesus returns to Nazareth after	Jan. 14 of 1 B.C.

<u>WHY DECEMBER 25TH</u>?

Early Christians actually celebrated December 25th before Rome began celebrating Dec. 25th as Christ's Birth. The Roman holiday Saturnalia, or *natalis solis invicti*, the birth of the sun god

(Nimrod), goes back to the Babylonian priesthood, and is recorded being celebrated as early as 274 A.D., by Rome.

Constantine required December 25th to be recognized for Christ's birth, along with all gods of the sun (Nimrod), in 313 A.D. The first recorded December 25th date for Christ's birth is listed as 336 A.D. in a Roman Almanac, according to Chuck Freas. Dr. Chuck Missler states it is first recorded in 354 A.D., in a calendar of Philocalus. The Christian church bishops formally adopted December 25th in 440 A.D.

But, Christians had already associated December 25th with the birth of Christ much earlier than all these dates for a completely different reason, according to William Tighe, Professor of History at Muhlenberg College. The December 25th date related to the Jewish tradition of the great prophets having an "integral age," where their day of death was also, either their day of birth, or conception. Jesus' death is dated to March 25th, and the feast of Passover. Early Christians celebrated March 25th as the Feast of Annunciation (His Conception), which would put His birth at December 25th. Also, December 25th would be remembered as the date the magi in Jerusalem saw the star stand still over Bethlehem.

The Babylonian practices, including the celebration of December 25th, and the birth of the sun god (Nimrod), were passed on to the church by Constantine, when he was pushing the Roman Empire to convert to Christianity. These Babylonian practices include the sacred traditions of the mother/child cult of Semiramis (known in various nations as Ishtar, Ashtaroth, Isis etc.), and her child Tammuz (Ezek. 8:14, Jer. 44:17-19 – see the Study on *The Queen of Heaven*--Target Truth Ministries.com).

In the beginning was the Zodiac, a story in the heavens, created by God, about His plan of salvation. The story involved a virgin, and a child who was to redeem those who would trust in Him (142, 143). This redemption story of the Zodiac became perverted, as men endeavored to take control, and be worshiped themselves. Worship for these various nations centered around a woman and child, a copy or imitation of God's plan. The earliest of these mother/child cults began with Nimrod and Babylon (Gen. 10:8-9), only a couple of generations after Noah and the flood. Nimrod, "*marad*," means "he rebelled," and the Babylonians built the tower of Babel. Nimrod set himself up as god and had priests cater to him.

Nimrod, after his death, was worshiped as the sun god (Baal). Nimrod had a queen Semiramis (the moon goddess – Semiramis is also known as Baal-Ti, or "my lady," or in Latin, as Mea Dominain, or in Italian, as Madonna). After Nimrod's death, Semiramis (Baal-Ti), became pregnant, supposedly from a sunbeam (from Baal – the sun god – Nimrod), and she gave birth to Tammuz, who was presented to the people as the reborn (resurrected), Nimrod. When Tammuz died, he was supposedly resurrected 40 days later. Semiramis introduced Tammuz as the promised savior (Gen. 3:15). Both mother and child were worshiped, and God's Zodiac story had now been forever perverted. From this myth, false worship of the mother goddess and child, came Babylon's religious practices.

When the nations scattered (Gen. 11:9), they formed various new nations, with various new languages, and variations of this mother/child cult developed around the world in Egypt, with Osiris (Nimrod), and Isis (Semiramis), and their child Horas (Tammuz). Historian, Herodotus, recorded how the ancient Babylonian rites began being practiced in various nations around the world, as did Hislop (113), Leyard (134, 135), Woodrow (132), and Bailey (133). Even in the *Catholic Encyclopedia* (136), Vol. 14, pages 515ff, and Vol. 15, pages 450ff, it is noted that these practices pre-date the Christian Church. These religious practices were eventually adopted by the Roman Empire when it came into power before Christ was even born. A few hundred years after Christ, these ancient Babylonian practices found their way into the Christian Church, because the Roman emperor desired to unite pagan Babylonian practices, and the Christian Church, into a single religion for the empire. This, of course, seemed a natural fit, as Mary and her Son (Jesus), matched well with the mother goddess and child pagan cults of most nations. Of course, Mary was never elevated to worshipful status by the early Christians. The elevation of Mary happened several hundred years after Christ died, due to the Roman emperor's desire to unite under one set of religious practices, which included the worship of the Queen of Heaven.

Some of these *symbols and practices from Babylon*, which after 300 years found their way into the Christian Church, include:

- Elevation of the mother, the virgin, to Queen, or Goddess–co-equal to God (Mary—see *Queen of Heaven*—Target Truth Ministries.com).
- Lighting of candles, used to signify the sun god of light(Nimrod).
- Prayer beads, used to count, and repeat, prayers to the Queen of Heaven.
- Resurrection of Nimrod as Tammuz is celebrated at Ishtar (Easter).
- Birth of Nimrod is celebrated on December 25th.
- Forty days of lent, prior to Ishtar (Easter), were practiced in recognition of the death, and resurrection, of Nimrod as Tammuz (Ezek. 8 :14; Jer. 44:17-19).
- Purgatory is a place where the dead await purification, and dates back to these Babylonian pagan beliefs, which pre-date Christianity.
- The later Babylonians worshiped the "mother" by making an offering as a memorial to Heras (the Queen of Heaven – the Moon Goddess. Hera was the equivalent to Eve of the Bible to the Greeks – the mother of all – see *Queen of Heaven* Study – <u>Greece</u> - Target Truth Ministries.com).
- The *cross*, the mystic Tau (the symbol of Tammuz), is used by Babylon to symbolize *man's power* over death. To Christians, the **cross** represents God's love (being willing to suffer the curse for us), *God's power* over death (1 Cor. 1:17-18).
- Babylonian priests were to be celibate, and virgin women who wore crosses around their necks, were to attend the priests. The Roman emperor, Constantine, combined the cultic practices with Christian worship, and in 378 A.D., Demasus, the Bishop of Rome, was crowned Pontifus Maximus (High Priest of Mysteries of the bridge between the dead and living, from the Babylonian tradition). Even at this date, most bishops didn't recognize the pope in Rome

as the authority of the church. In Rome, was not recognized until around 1000 A.D., and even then the Eastern Church still did not recognize the authority of the pope in Rome. This is still true today. Today, the pope's crown is an exact replica of the Babylonian priest's crown—a fish head—Dagon (143).

Many ancient myths, which seemed to parallel the story of Christ (virgin birth, resurrection etc.), were elevated to historical status in the late 1800's, and the early 1900's. Recent scholarship has, however, shown each of these fall far short of being historic parallels. Lee Strobel (59) has provided evidence showing these myths have been either later embellished to relate to Christ, or were actually created after the time of Christ. Historically, these myths in no way even closely relate to the life of Christ. We must remember the original story of the virgin and the resurrection, were actually given in the Zodiac by God, and it has been perverted into these other myths.

Back to the birth of Christ, the Eastern Catholic Church celebrate the birth of Christ on the 6th of January, the 12th day of Christmas, and they believe there were twelve magi.

MICHAELMAS: September 29th. This is the date celebrated for centuries in Europe as the true day of Christ's birth. December 25th, was actually banned in Europe because of its link to Babylon. Even the Pilgrims in America banned December 25th and celebrated the date of September 29th (see the "Why December 25th?" discussion).

REVELATION 12: In 3 B.C., and 2 B.C., in September, at the Feast of Trumpets, on the horizon, one would see the picture described by John, in Revelation 12, of a women clothed in the sun, standing on the moon (142). The woman (constellation Virgo), just above the moon with the sun, in Virgo. To the Magi, this either (in 3 B.C. or 2 B.C.), would indicate the birth of a king, and confirm their understanding. For John, this image could be what God had prepared for the world (Magi), to recognize as the Messiah's birth, but it also represents Israel, God's chosen (a part of the woman—all the betrothed — 142), standing on the moon, the image of false worship (see next section on *Islam*).

The woman (Israel and all the betrothed--142), is about to give birth to the Messiah, who would be the source of salvation for the whole world. The name Jesus means "salvation." Note that neither Herod, nor the priests, knew anything about what the star (or event) the Magi saw, as astrology is forbidden for Israel (Matt. 2:4).

September 29, 2 B.C.: at the Feast of Trumpets, is the most likely date for the birth of Christ, considering the available evidence.

References (113 – 119)

Six hundred years after the resurrection of Jesus from death, Christianity was spreading to the East, until another major force came into being…Islam.

ISLAM & PROPHECY

See *Target Truth Ministries.com*
for News & Updates

A RABS...All are descendants of Abraham—Nomads. *Not* all are Islamic. Over one million Arabs are Christians, and even Christian Arabs call God Allah, the name of God in Arabic. Most are from Ishmael (second wife, Hagar—Egyptian). Some are from Esau, Jacob's brother (first wife, Sarai). Some are from Keturah (third wife of Abraham). Note that most Arabs in "Palestine," prior to Mohammed, were Christians or Jewish, even though many Arab tribes continued to worship many gods, because of their heritage (see *The Fertile Crescent Timeline* Study—144). Palestine Arabs worshiped one God, whereas, many tribes outside the influence of Palestine worshiped many gods (until Mohammed established one main god, 600 years after Jesus).

ISLAM: Not to be confused with Arab people. Only fifteen percent of Islam are Arab people. Islam is a religion founded by Mohammed, who received a vision, in a cave, from an angel, exactly like the Mormon Joseph Smith (Gal. 1:8-9). The penalty for leaving Islam is death. (See the *Truth Matrix*—Target Truth Ministries.com).

ORIGIN: Islam is the worship of the moon god Sin (2000 B.C., 2,500 years *before* Mohammed), which means the controller of night, known to Islam as the moon god Hubal, or Al-ilah, which was the main god of Ur of the Chaldees (Abraham, Gen. 11:28).

Dr. Morey states: "Islam is a modern version of one of the ancient fertility cults. The Allah of the Qur'an is not the same as the God of the Bible, and the religion of Abraham is not derived from paganism." Alfred Guilaume states: "The other gods mentioned in the Qur'an are all female deities: Al-Lat, Al-Uzza, and Manat, which represented the sun, the planet Venus, and Fortune, respectively. At Mecca, they were regarded as the daughters of Allah. As Allah meant 'the god,' so Al-lat means 'the goddess.'" John Van Ess states: "At Mecca Allah was the chief of the gods and the special deity of the Quaraish, the prophet's tribe. Allah had three daughters: Manah, the goddess of destiny, Al-lat, the goddess of vegetable life, and Hubal (moon god), and more than 300 others made up the pantheon." G.J.O. Moshay states: "The word Allah was derived from Al-ilah, which had become a generic title for whatever god was considered the highest god. Each Arab tribe used Allah to refer to its own particular high god. This is why Hubal, the moon god (Sin), was the central focus of prayer at the Ka'aba, and the people prayed to Hubal (Sin), using the name Allah." Historians like Vaqqidi have said Allah was actually the leader of the 360 gods being worshipped in Arabia at the time Mohammed rose in prominence. Ibn Al-Kabi gave 27 names of pre-Islamic deities. Interestingly, not many Muslims want to accept that Allah was already being worshipped at the Ka'aba in Mecca by Arab pagans *before Mohammed* came."

The moon god Sin was common to many cultures all over the world, long before Mohammed, and can be traced all the way back to Nimrod, and Babylon – 2000 B.C. In Rome, Diana was the moon god (1,000 years before Mohammed), the daughter of Jupiter, and Diana was a virgin, controller of childbirth, and resurrection. Her symbol was a crescent moon. The moon god Sin (2000 B.C.), commonly called by Arabs Hubal, was considered the highest of gods, or Al-ilah.

The mythical origin of the entire universe was due to Nanmu, the water goddess. From her waters was birthed all we see (an imitation—Gen. 1:6). One of these births was the moon god Sin (male). Sin was transformed to a female goddess as a result of the earth goddess Inanna, becoming Queen of Heaven, as well as Queen of

Earth, due to her marring many other gods, including Anu (104 pg. 78, 81). She became the moon goddess with resurrection power, thus, replacing the male god Sin. As time passed, the moon goddess, combined with Isis (Egypt), and became known as Namaia. Eventually, male dominance caused a return to the worship of the moon god Sin (male), or Al-ilah, the primary god of many of the Arab tribes, including Mohammed's. Al-ilah was the primary god of the Ka'aba in Mecca, as well as Ur, where Abraham came from (and where Abraham was called out of– See Gen. 12:1).

Mohammed received a revelation while under great physical stress from an angel (see Mormon also – Gal. 1:8-9), and Mohammed proclaimed the moon god Sin (Hubal), known as Al-ilah to the Arab tribes, to be the one true god—Allah. Daniel 11:37 denotes that Allah (the "so-called" god of Abraham), is not the same as the true God of Moses. Today, both witchcraft and Islam share the exact same symbol – a crescent moon with a star. In Satanism and witchcraft, Lucifer is lower than the moon god. This is true also of Islam.

The black cube in Mecca (Ka'aba – most holy site), was to honor all the gods, and primarily the moon god Allah (Al-ilah). A believer is called Moslem (Muslim). The goal of Islam is to overtake the whole world for Allah (see quotations from Quran), peacefully or force- fully, to overtake the Jew and the Christian who pervert their god. Islam is *not* to be confused with Arabs, many of which are Christian. Twelve million Americans are Muslims. If only one half of one percent are radical, that means there are 50,000 extremists in America. Louis Farrakhan, the leader of Nation Islam, here in the United States, is considered by many to be very extreme, and his group claims up to one million followers. Louis Farrakhan claims to have met with Mohammed when he was transported to the "mother ship" which exists above our earth. They claim the Jewish people actually caused 9-11.

<u>MECCAN CHRONICLES</u>: from Mohammed's period, state that all Jews are to be annihilated.

<u>QURAN</u>	5:82	Jews are the main enemy of Islam.
	5:51	Jews and Christians are defiled filth and not to be trusted.
	2:61	Jews are vileness, and are separated from Allah.
	3:112	The just reward for Jews is destruction.
	3:156-159	Those who die during a Jihad (holy war), are martyrs and receive immediate entrance into paradise (4:74-76, 9:88-89, 111 – 12:58-59, 61:4, 9-13).
	3:167-175	To be a martyr is the ultimate show of submission and devotion to Allah.
	5:51	To take a Christian or Jew for a friend is to offend Allah.
	9:112	The Umma (true believer of Islam), has the promise of Allah, written in the blood of the moon, that paradise comes to those who kill and are killed in a holy war.

ISLAM

A religion of peace for Islamic countries, referred to as the "House of peace", as opposed to the "House of war" for all others. Islam has been misused by some people who see it as a religion of peace for all people, when it is the duty of Muslims to convert people to Islam, or rule them as sub- human.
Qur'an Sura 5:33, 5:51, 8:67, 9:5, 9:29, 47:4, 98:6 **Hadith** 4-52-196, 4-53-386, 4-53- 392, 8-82-705

Fundamental elements of Islam are that Muhammad is not tolerant. Muhammad is patient. Muslims are called to be patient until they can intervene in this life.

Muslims believe they are correct. Muslims believe others are lost, and going to hell.

Fundamental Muslims ARE called to force or coerce conversion to the fundamental.

To tolerate Christian or Jewish groups in society, is to invite the **sword**. Muslims are taught that the later teachings of Muhammad (Jihad), override the early teachings of peace, and co-existence.

CHRISTIANITY

A religion of peace, both for those in Christianity, and those not. Christianity has been misused by some people to try and force people to convert. Christians are to respect a person's right to reject God. It is their right to deny God, and receive hell in the next life. **Matthew 5, 6, 7**

Fundamental elements of Christianity are that Jesus is not tolerant. Jesus is patient. Christians are called to be patient until Jesus intervenes, in the judgment at the end.

Christians believe they are correct. Christians believe others are going to hell.

Fundamental Christians are NOT called to force or coerce conversion to the fundamental.

To tolerate fundamental Islam groups in society, is to invite **debate**. Christians are not to use force, only warn the world of the judgment to come. Judgment will be carried out by Christ alone.

Instruct a person they must follow Allah, and the Islamic laws, or they will be punished with death in this life, and hell in the next.
Qur'an Sura 5:33, 47:4, 98:6

Instruct a person they must follow Jesus (**John 14:6**), and the ways of Jesus, or they will be punished with eternal hell in life to come – **Matt. 28:16-20**, and suffer a lack of peace of mind in this life (**John 14:6**).

The government is to be controlled by the law of Islam. Arabic must be the language of the world. Peace treaties must expire in 10 years maximum, and used only to strengthen the Islamic position.

The government, laws are to be submitted to by the Christian. If the laws are opposed to the teachings of Jesus, then a Christian is to accept punishment, rather than deny God. (**Matt. 22:21, Mk. 12:17, Rom. 13, 1 Pet. 2:13-16**). Jesus established the laws for Christians – **Matt. 5,6,7,15**

Law – Based upon the Quran, and using the example of Muhammad, as laid out in the Hadith and <u>interpreted by the religious leaders</u>, will be the law of the governments for all Islamic Nations.

Law – Whatever laws are established by the <u>local governments</u>. Christians are to submit, even if Islam. BUT-see govern

To deny Allah, or deny Islam, or deny the Islamic laws, is to show yourself to be sub-human, and subject to being killed, as one would kill an ape, or pig, and hell, thereafter.
Qur'an Sura 5:33, 5:51, 8:67, 9:5, 9:29, 47:4, 98:6
Hadith 4-52-196, 4-53-386, 4-53-392, 8-82-705

To deny Jesus, and God's laws, is to separate oneself from the kingdom of God, and to be subject to eternal separation, which Jesus (not man) will carry out in the judgment to come.
Mark 9:43

Islam has no evidence of any power over death. Islam is a philosophy of how to live in this world, with no evidence to support their view of life after death.

Christianity has fulfilled prophecies and eyewitness evidence of hundreds of people, on several occasions, over many weeks, seeing Jesus returning from the dead, and promising that those who trust in Him will be received into His kingdom, and others sent to hell.
1 Cor. 15:1-8, Acts 1:1-8

Example – adultery – Sex outside of marriage, or homosexual relations is forbidden.
Punishment – Requires head to be severed.
Hadith 2-23-413

Adultery – Sex outside of marriage, or homosexual relations is forbidden
Matt.15:17-20
Punishment may be none, or is determined by the local government. Christians are to be admonished by the Church they belong to, and if not repentant, they will suffer eternal separation, which will be administered by Jesus (not man) at the final judgment to come.
Mk. 9:43-44

Example – Lying – To protect Islam, it is Example – Lying – Obey whatever acceptable to lie. Otherwise, it is not government laws are established. OK to lie.
Punishment – Whatever the Muslim leader establishes in the district you live in.
Quran Sura 3:28, 16:106
Hadith 4-52-269, 7-67-427

Punishment – Christians are to be admonished by the church, and. if not repentant, eternal separation will be administered by Jesus at the judgment to come.
Matt. 15, 19, John 5:28-29

161

ISLAMIC TRADITION from Mohammed is that the complete military subjugation of the earth is commanded by Allah (see Islam Prophecy). Also, the tradition from the thirteenth century, after the twelfth Imam disappeared in 974 AD, is that the twelfth Imam (the Mahdi), will return, and establish Islam as the global religion, and he will reign for *seven years* before bringing about the end of the world.

- The twelfth Imam (the Mahdi), will return to convert the world to Islam. The Sunnis basically believe that he is either yet to be born, or may be alive already, and has not yet emerged, or been revealed. The Shiites believe the Mahdi (the twelfth Imam), was hidden by Muhammad until an appointed time. There is a holy well where messages can be left for the Imam, and today, some expect the Iman (the Mahdi), to emerge from this well. The leaders of Iran in 2005, announced that they expected this to happen during the 2009–2012 timeframe (some believe this was actually fulfilled on 2-14-2012 and that the end-times are now here).
- A false messiah, a Jew, will lead an army against Islam.
- Many Shiites and Sunnis say the prophet Jesus (Jesus is seen by these to escort the twelfth Imam), will be sent by Mohammed, will return to defeat the Jewish army, and Islam will become the sole faith and power, and Jerusalem will become the new Islamic capital.
- Islam expects the Jewish people to attack Al-Aqsa, a Temple Mount worship area at the south end of the Temple mount in Jerusalem.
- Muslim tradition teaches that the final judgment of all humankind will take place in the Kidron Valley between the Dome of the Rock (Temple Mount – Moriah), and the Mount of Olives on the east side of Jerusalem.

ISLAMIC PROPHECY from the thirteenth century predicted the end of the world would be ushered in only after three things occurred:

1) The Jews would control Palestine (Israel lost control 2,500 years ago and regained control in 1948, and in 1967 regained control over Jerusalem). *This has happened!*
2) Only after the Byzantines invade Hijaz (said to have been fulfilled when America, seen as the Byzantines (the West), entered Kuwait and northern Saudi Arabia, the area of Hijaz in the 1990's). *This has happened!*
3) Only after the Jews occupy Al-Aqsa on the Temple Mount (still to happen). See Study *"The Third Temple*--Target Truth Ministries.com.

After these things, the Mahdi (the twelfth Imam), will destroy the Jew and Christian, and will establish Islam as the global religion, and he will reign for *seven years* before bringing about the end of the world.

Only after these have occurred, then will the Holy Qur'an be fulfilled, by the Jew being conquered and destroyed. Islam regards the Bible as a corrupted record of God's revelation. Islam sees the Qur'an as the correct revelation, and says the Qur'an has foretold of the Jew being in the land, and then being destroyed, and this is to be accomplished by Islam.

Islamic prophecy states the Christian anti-Christ will actually be a future Jewish messiah (not Jesus). Islamic prophecy states we are in the last 120 years of this earth age. The end will be in the year 1,500 on the Islamic calendar...2076 on the western calendar (120). The last days then, for Islam, began in 1956, exactly in the midst of 1948 and 1967. On or before the year 2076, Islam expects that many living will see Jesus, or the twelfth Imam (Mahdi), return to the earth, to conquer the Jews and Christians in the final holy war, and establish Islam as the rule of the earth. The year 2006 for Islam saw the last generation born before the end (as a generation is 70 years), and it is the duty of this generation to finish the command of Allah, and eliminate the Christian and Jewish presence. Present-day Islamic teachings state that Ezekiel 38:5-6 confirms that Iran/ Persia, is to lead the assault on Israel – Iran is the first country listed by God in this passage.

<u>5 Pillars of Faith</u>:

1) One God, Allah. Jesus was created (is not God). The term "Son of God" refers to his being a physical creation, and is not a reference to the Trinity (Father, Jesus, Holy Spirit). Also, he did not die on the cross, someone else did. But, Jesus was taken to heaven like Enoch and Elijah. The Holy Spirit is the angel Gabriel (see Message *"God, or Son of God, or Son of Man, or What?* Target Truth Ministries.com.

2) Pray five times a day (Shia pray three times). Face Mecca (they used to face Jerusalem until 622 A.D.). Women must worship separately. When Mohammed was in Mecca in the early years of his teaching, he taught peace and prayer facing Jerusalem. When he was forced out of Mecca, by other tribes after thirteen years, he went to Medina in 622 A.D., and changed his position from peace, to oppression against those who would not accept him as the prophet of God, including Christians, Jews, and other Arab tribes. Prayer was now to face Mecca. Most "Palestinian" Arabs were actually Christian until 622 A.D. when persecuted.

3) Give two-and-a-half percent of earnings to help people and strangers—the purification tax. Do good. Man is not born sinful. Man is born good, but weak, and must do good works. A person will prosper if he does enough good work.

4) Fast during one month of Ramadan, from sunrise to sunset. To this day, the faithful fast during the month which begins and ends with the appearance of the crescent moon in the sky.

5) Once in a lifetime, do the Hajj to Mecca and the Ka'aba.

One must cut their hair, wear white clothes, no jewelry, and bathe. They are to circle the Ka'aba three times running, four times walking, and throw seven pebbles (or 7x7 – 49), at the three stone pillars, which represent Satan's temptations of Abraham. Then, kiss the Black Stone, because Muhammad did it, and because the Black Stone removes sins. Adam was given a white stone when he was forced out of Paradise, and it has turned black, by taking the sins of pilgrims away as they kiss it. At the end of the pilgrimage, there is a feast of sacrifice – a blood sacrifice, as a reminder of Genesis 22 and the story of Abraham sacrificing Ishmael (not Isaac – Sura 37:102,112). Tradition is that Adam and Eve built the Ka'aba, and it was restored by Abraham and Ishmael.

<u>Five Articles of Faith</u> (Some say six, the sixth being God's Decree):

1) Allah is the greatest god.
2) Angels are instruments of God's will.
3) Holy Book is the <u>Qur'an</u>, an updated Bible. The Qur'an respects the Bible, but claims the Bible was corrupted by Jewish people. The Qur'an was revealed to Muhammad over a period of 22 year from 610-632 A.D. In 650 A.D., the third Caliph established the text of the Qur'an which exists today. Sura 16:101 reads Allah can change his revelations. Sura 41:9-10, 12 reads Allah took eight days to create the world, and Sura 50:38 reads creating humans took six days.
4) There are 28 prophets of Allah, including Moses and Jesus, and Muhammad was the last.
5) There is a judgment, and hell.

<u>The Hadith</u>: Note that the text which is used to interpret the Qur'an is called the Hadith. The Hadith is said to amplify the Qur'an, because it quotes the actual words and actions of Muhammad. Muslims follow the example of Muhammad laid out in the Hadith. The Qur'an is said by Islam to be ambiguous without the Hadith. The Hadith was put together around 860 A.D. by Sahih-Al-Bukhari, 200 years after Muhammad's death.

- 4:177 – The end times and peace will not come until the Jews are subdued.
- Hadith says the only assured way to Paradise is to die in Jihad, a holy war. Otherwise, there is no guarantee. Even if one keeps all the 5 pillars, Allah may still overlook you. Those that overcome suffering, and are purified in hell, *may* be acceptable to Paradise, but there is still no assurance.

- Hell contains mostly women.
- Those who commit suicide, not as a result of Jihad, will stay in hell for all eternity.
- Muhammad taught that women were less intelligent. Women are not considered inferior, but dangerous, and therefore, must be controlled.
- Women must worship separately.
- Women must cover their hair, as hair is an object of sexual temptation (1 Cor. 11:10 – angels — 141).
- Women can marry one Muslim man; whereas, men can marry up to 4 women, and they can be non-Muslim.
- Women cannot divorce; whereas, men can.
- In Paradise, men can have many companions, otherwise, women mostly would stay in hell.

7th Heaven:

The term "seventh heaven" is associated with Islam, but originates with Aristotle, in 300 B.C., and refers to the seven crystal spheres, with earth at the center, the sun, moon, four planets, and the sphere of the stars.

Major Groups:

Sunnis: Eighty-five percent of Islam (Egypt's major group). They accept the leadership and authority of the first three Caliphs (beginning with the close companion, and father-in-law of Muhammad, Abu Bakr. The last Caliph, Uthman, was assassinated in 656 A.D.), and later on, the authority transferred to the Umayyad Dynasty in Damascus, which took over the line of Caliphs, which existed until 1924, through the Ottoman Empire. They believe salvation comes from being part of the greater community of faith. A group, not an individual, exercises control and reveals truth. Al-Qaeda is basically Sunni, with connections to Wahhabis.

Shiites: Ten percent of Islam (Iran's major group). They follow their Imam to receive salvation. The Imams come from the bloodline of succession, belonging to the family of the prophet Muhammad, beginning with Muhammad's cousin Ali (who was assassinated). The twelfth and final Imam disappeared, and is expected to return in the end times (see the sections on Islamic Tradition, and Islamic Prophecy). Today, a council of leaders elects a supreme leader, called the Ayatollah, and they receive their revelations from caba- lists involved in channeling and occultation. The leader interprets. Marriage can be temporary. Hezbollah and Hamas are Shia, with connections to Wahhabis.

<u>Sufis</u>: One percent of Islam (found mainly in Iraq). They trace their roots to Zoroaster, which taught that a future king from the line of Abraham would raise the dead. Muhammad was the prophet, but not the king which they are waiting for. They receive their understanding of God through direct mystical revelation to each individual.

<u>Alawites</u>: Less than one percent (found mainly in Syria). They believe in reincarnation, in addition to Allah.

<u>Takfirs</u>: Less than one percent (found mainly in Kuwait). They lean toward materialism and positivism as good ideals, and (begin- ning with the close companion, and father-in-law of Muhammad, Abu Bakr. The last Caliph, Uthman, was assassinated in 656 A.D.), and later on, the authority transferred to the Umayyad Dynasty in Damascus, which took over the line of Caliphs, which existed until 1924, through the Ottoman Empire. They believe salvation comes from being part of the greater community of faith. A group, not an individual, exercises control and reveals truth. Al-Qaeda is basi- cally Sunni, with connections to Wahhabis.

<u>Wahhabis</u>: Less than one percent (found mainly in Saudi Arabia). They lean toward being practical and reasoning, and see themselves as the generation called to fulfill Islamic prophecy, and are the pri- mary source of radical Islam, and Jihad today, with connections to many other groups.

Indonesia is the largest country (150 million), followed by Pakistan (140 million), Bangladesh, India, Turkey, USSR, Egypt, Iran, Nigeria, Iraq (16 million), USA (11 million).

References (104, 120 – 130, 137-140)

Ancient civilizations had great knowledge. Ancient civilizations had a common connection to God's plan of salvation (the Zodiac — 142, 143). But, ancient civilizations also allowed God's plan to be subverted.

Even if most people in the Western countries think all this prophecy stuff is a waste of time, one must remember that in Islam, they live to fulfill it. It is Satan's plan to separate us from God. Satan is the great imitator, and will offer peace to the world, if we will trust in him and ignore Christ. Satan gives people many alternatives other than Jesus. Science can also be used to separate people from God, but science does not need to be one of the persuasions in Satan's bag of tricks, unless we ignore some of the scientific evidence, and embrace theories without solid evidence to support them. Let us study _all_ the evidence.

For more information see News & Updates at
Target Truth Ministries.com

APPENDIX

EARTH TIME CHART: Science, Origins, & Ancient Civilizations

APPENDIX   AGE   Part A

CONVENTIONAL SCIENTIFIC HYPHOTISIS

4.5 Billion years ago – Earth is forming as a molten ball of fire. Granite forms as the building base rock of all the continents. Seas form, possibly as a result of comets bringing water to the new planet from above.

3.5 Billion years ago – Life in water leaves deposits called Stromatolites

1.0 Billion years ago – Granite formations become one giant barren rocky land mass which science calls Rhodinia.

700 Million years ago – Earth cools and becomes an ice ball, and only bacteria and algae can live. Oxygen is forming.

650 Million years ago – Ice becomes one mile thick over the whole Earth. The surface temperature becomes minus 40 degrees.

530 Million years ago – Volcanism causes ice to breakup, oxygen increases, and an explosion of life occurs. All life forms emerge in this Cambrian era. This single land mass, with life, is now called Pangaea by science.

400 Million years ago – Oxygen increases, and Ozone forms, which protects life from the Sun's harmful ultraviolet light.

300 Million years ago – Carboniforus era – trees and jungles form todays coal deposits. Insects rule, and oxygen levels rise. Amphibians develop, followed later on by reptiles.

GOD'S WORD

The Land (singular)
Gen. 1:9
The Sea – Gen. 1:7-9
Vegetation
Gen. 1:11-12
Sea Life
Gen. 1:20-21
Birds – Gen. 1:20-21
Animals – Gen. 1:24-25
Humans – Gen. 1:27

250 Million Years ago – 95% of life species go extinct due to the Siberian mantle eruption, vulcanization, and poisonous gases escaping.

180 Million years ago – Continents continue to split, and increasing carbon dioxide causes global warming, resulting in tropical forests, even at the poles.

150 Million years ago – Life evolved to dinosaurs as oxygen increases, and life from this era forms todays oil deposits. Earth's magnetic field keeps declining, and needs recharging.

65 Million years ago – 75% of all species go extinct, including the dinosaurs, as a result of a meteor impact. A meteor triggers volcanic activity and toxic dust. Core reversals recharge the magnetic field.

50 Million years ago – Mammals begin to flourish. The worlds great mountain ranges form as continents, and Earth's plates, collide.

6 Million years ago – Grand Canyon is being up-lifted, and eroded, at the same time. Earth's magnetic field looses strength, and needs recharging frequently. Earth's magnetic field is recharged by core reversals.

2 Million years ago – Ice age begins, and man emerges from Africa / Near East. Ice age is caused by sea currents being disrupted by the formation of Panama. Ice in New York is as high as the Empire State Building. Earth's magnetic field is recharged every so often by core reversals.

TODAY – Lands are moving slowly, but could move massively. Note that God's Word tells us that the earth broke up dramatically over an 1,800 year period. The basic difference between the science based on evidence, and the science based on theory, is **time and age** of the earth and life. A short time frame points to a Creator God, which is not acceptable to the conventional community of theoretic science. (see the books in this series, ***Science, Origins & Ancient Civilizations***, at burneyfam.com).

The Flood – all die, and Earth broken (2,550 BC) **Gen. 7:11**
Noah and family land and migrate from Near-East in various directions.

Earth is further divided
Peleg (2,380 BC)
Gen. 10:25
People migrate to all parts of earth – **Gen. 11:8**

Earth is further divided
Joshua 10:13-14 (1400 BC)
Isaiah 24:1, 19
Major Earth movements
Isaiah 38:8 (701 BC)
(701 BC – the world's calendars go from 360 days to 365)

APPENDIX   AGE   Part B

GOD'S WORD

The Land (singular)
Gen. 1:9
The Sea – **Gen. 1:7-9**
Vegetation
Gen. 1:11-12
Sea Life
Gen. 1:20-21
Birds – **Gen. 1:20-21**
Animals – **Gen. 1:24-25**
Humans – **Gen. 1:27**

ACTUAL SCIENTIFIC EVIDENCE

* Granite must form in a cold state. To this day, no one knows how the granite formed, and no one knows where the water came from.

* Stromatolites are lumps, or lobes, of rock, and these are still being deposited even today.

* All science agrees that the land was originally one large mass (the **Bible** also agrees).

* Science is split on previous ice ages. Some say yes, yes, some say no. Earth was supposedly still to hot for ice to form, according to many scientists.

* Fossil evidence shows all life types in this Cambrian sedimentary layer. Sedimentary layers are formed by water deposition, containing no radiometric dating material.

* Science agrees that oxygen levels in the past were higher, but there are no fossils which show evolution. Fossils of same kind are found in more than one layer. These layers have no radiometric dating material to determine age.

The Flood – all die, and
Earth broken (2,550 BC)
Gen. 7:11
Noah and family land and
migrate from Near-East
in various directions.

Earth is further divided
Peleg (2,380 BC)
Gen. 10:25
People migrate to all
parts of earth – **Gen. 11:8**

* All science agrees on the land splitting up. The argument is over the time scale, and whether global warming, or crustal displacement, caused the vegetation which is buried under the ice at the poles.

* There is no evidence of Macro-evolution in the fossil record, only Micro-evolution within species. Even today, dinosaur bones are not yet fossilized, and reveal testable DNA.

* These meteor impacts, along with the earth's crust breaking up, could explain why the earth's magnetic field keeps recharging. The iridium layer exists all over the earth. Science agrees mountain ranges are the result of continental movement.

Earth is further divided
Joshua 10:13-14 (1400 BC)
Isaiah 24:1, 19
Major Earth movements
Isaiah 38:8 (701 BC)
(701 BC – the world's calendars go from 360 days to 365)

* Some scientists theorize the Grand Canyon is the result of great flooding. Some scientists believe the land moves slowly (millions of years). Others theorize that the earth's crust has moved massively due to crustal displacement, or Mars fly-bys, thus recharging the Earth's magnetic field. There is no evidence for core reversals.

* <u>TODAY</u> – Lands are moving slowly, but could move massively. Note that God's Word tells us that the earth broke up dramatically over an 1,800 year period. The basic difference between the science based on evidence, and the science based on theory, is <u>**time and age**</u> of the earth and life. A short time frame points to a Creator God, which is not acceptable to the conventional community of theoretic science. (see book *Science, Origins & Ancient Civilizations*)

172

REFERENCES

Target Truth Ministries.com

1. *Newsweek,* May 4, 1992:76.

2. Troitske, V. S., *Astrophysics and Space Science* 139 (1987).

3. Sutterfield, Barry, and Norman, Trevor, *Atomic Constants, Light and Time* (Flanders: University of South Australia, 1987).

4. Van Flandem,vT. C., "Is the Gravitational Constant Changing?" *Precision Measurements and Fundamental Constants II* (1984, 625-627.

5. Slusher, Harold S., "Traveling of Light in Space," *Age of the Cosmos* (San Diego: ICR, 1980), 25-37.

6. Humphreys, D. R., "Good News from Neptuen: The Voyager II Magnetic Measurements," Creation Research Society Quarterly (1990).

7. Zage, Wayne M., "*The Geometry of Binocular Visual Space,*" Mathematics Magazine, 53: 289-293.

8. Lord Kelvin, *Mathematical and Physical Papers,* (Cambridge University Press, 1911).

9. Slichter, Louis B., "*Secular Effects of Tidal Friction Upon the Earth's Rotation,*" Journal of Geographic Resources, Vol. 8, No. 14:4281-4288.

10. Witcomb, John C, and Donald B. DeYoung. *The Moon, Its Creation, Form and Significance*. (Winona Lake, Indiana, BMII Books 1978) 41

11. Lubkin, Gloria B., *Physics Today,*Vol. 32, no. 17.

12. Lerner, Eric, *"The Cosmologist's New Clothier,"* Sky and Telescope, No. 83, (1992), 124, and Geoffrey Burbridge, *"Why Only One Big Bang?"* Scientific American, Vol. 3, No. 266. (1992) 120.

13. Austin, Steven A., Geology from data from J. Woodmorapple, *"The Essential Nonexistence of the Evolutionary"* — uniformitarian geologic column: a quantitative assessment, Creation Research Society Quarterly, Vol. 18:46-71.

14. Ager, D. V., *The Nature of the Stratigraphical Record,* 2nd ed.:11.

15. Pettijohn, F. J., *Sedimentary Rocks,*.New York: Harper and Row, (1975) 334.

16. Fold, R. L. Fold, *"Practical Petrographic Classification of Limestones,"* American Association of Petroleum Geologists Bullitin, Vol. 43.

17. Rosenfeld, C. L., and G. L. Beach. *Remote Sensing Analysis, Mount St. Helens*. (Oregon State University Water Resources Research Institute).

18. Ager, D. V., *The Nature of the Stratigraphical Record,* 2nd ed.: 11.

19. Hammer, C. U., H. B. Clausen, W. Dansgaard, N. Gunderstrup, S. J. Johnsen, and N. Reech. *"Dating of Greenland Ice Cores by Flow Models,"* Isotopes, Volcanic Debris and Continental Dust.

20. Johnsen, S. J., W. Dansgaard, and H. B. Clausen, *"Oxygen Isotope Profiles Throughout the Antarctic and Greenland Ice Sheets,"* Nature Vol. 288:230.

21. Paul, M. A., "*The supraglacial Land-system,*" <u>Glacial Geology</u>, 71-90.

22. Tissot, B. P., and D. H. Welte. *Petroleum Bormation and Occurrence,* 409:410.

23. DiNello, R. K., and C. K. Chang, *Isolation and Modification of Natural Porphyrius* 328.

24 Rupke, N. A., "*Sedimentary Evidence for the Allochthonous Origin of Stigmaria, carboninferious,* "<u>Geological Society of American Bulletin</u>, Vol. 40:62:73.

25. Price, P. H., "*Eratic Boulders in Sewell Coal,*" <u>Journal of Geology</u>, Vol. 40:56-73.

26. Hill, G. R., *Chemical Technology,* 296.

27. Lanzerotti, L. J., "*Measurement of the Large Scale Direct-Current Potential and Possible Implications for the Geomagnetic Dynamo,*" <u>Science,</u> Issur 229:47-49.

28. Humpherys, D. R., "*Has the Earth's Magnetic Field Ever Flipped?*" <u>Creation Research Society Quarterly</u> Issue 25 (1985).

29. Merril, R. T., and M. W. McElhinney, *The Earth's Magnetic Field.* (London: London Academic Press, 1983), 101-106.

30. Humpherys, Russell, Ph. D., Physics. Sandia National Laboratories, New Mexico (1992).

31. Bagenal, F., "*The Emptiest Magnetosphere,*" <u>Physics World</u>, (October 1989), 18-19.

32. Aardsma, Gerald A., Ph. D., Astro/Geophysics: research in accelerator mass spectrometry, University of Toronto.

33. McKee, F. H., and D. C. Noble, "*Age of the Cardenas Lavas, Grand Canyon,*" <u>Geological Society of America Bulletin</u>, Issue 87.

34. Gentry, R. V., *"Radio halos in coalified wood: new evidence relating to the time of uranium introduction and coalification,"* Science, Vol. 194:

315-318.

35. Turkevich, *Newsweek* (Dec. 1991).

36. Gentry, Robert, *Annual Review of Nuclear Science,* Vol. 23.

37. Jueneman, Frederick, *"Scientific Speculation,"* Industrial Research. Also: Duane Gish Ph. D., Biochemistry. University of Calif., Berkeley.

38. Anderson, J. L., and G. W. Spangler. *"Radiometric Dating : Is the Decay Constant?"* Pensee, Vol. 4, No 31 (1974).

39. Radio-carbon. Vol. 8.

40. Radio-carbon Vol. 10.

41. Antarctic Journal, Vol. 6:211.

42. Science, Vol. 141:634-637.

43. Science, Vol. 224:58-61.

44. Lee, R. E., *"Radio-carbon, Ages in Error,"* Anthropological Journal of Canada, Vol. 19, No. 3:9.

45. Kitts, David B., *"Paleontology and Evolutionary Theory,"* Evolution, Vol. 28.

46. Kelso, A. J., *Physical Anthropology* 2nd ed.:142 (1974).

47. Zukerman, Sir Solly, *Beyond the Ivory Tower,* New York: Taplinger Publishing Company, 1970, 64.

48. Ivanhoe, Francis, *"Was Virchow Right About Neanderthal?"* Nature, Vol. 227:577.

49. Eckhardt, Robert B., *"Population Genetics and Human Origins,"* Scientific American, Vol. 226:94, 101.

50. Oxnard, Charles E., *"Human Fossils: New Views of Old Bones,"* American Biology Teacher, Vol. 41:264.

51. Strass, William L., *Science,* Vol. 119:265, and William K. Gregory, *Science,* Vol. 66, 579 (1954).

52. Raup, D., *"Conflicts Between Darwin and Paleontology,"* Field Museum of Natural History Bulletin 50:25.

53. Bruce, Les, Ph. D., Linguistics, and David Thomas, Summer Institute of Linguistics (1995).

54. Elgin, Suzette H., *What is Linguistics?* (Englewood Cliffs: New Jersey, Prentice-Hall, 1973).

55. Levinton, Jeffery, *"The Big Bang of Animal Evolution,"* Scientific American (Nov. 1992) 84-91.

56. Lyttleton, R. A., *Mysteries of the Solar System* (Oxford: Clarendon Press).

57. Cook, M. A., *"Race Gas Absorption of Solids of the Lunar Regolith,"* Journal of Colloid and Interface Science, Vol. 38, No. 1

58. Cook, Melvin A., *"Where is the Earth Radiogenic Helium?"* Nature, Vol. 179:213.

59. Faul, H., *Nuclear Geology* (New York: John Wiley, 1954).

60. Koltz, J.W., *Genes, Genesis and Evolution,* (St. Louis: Concordia Publishing) 208.

61. Simpson, G., *The History of Life,* pg. 117, 149 and also, *Evolution After Darwin* (Chicago: University of Chicago Press, 1960) 143-144.

62. Cook, M. A., *Prehistory and Earth Models* (London: Max Parrish).

63. Blick, E. F., *"Mathematical Modeling of the Evidence for the Origin of Deep-Earth Hydrocarbons,"* IASTED International Symposium, Lugano, Switzerland. June 18-19, 1990.

64. Slusher, Harold S., *Age of the Earth from Some Astronomical Indicators,* unpublished; see also: *Age of the Cosmos.*

65. Clementson, S. P., *"A Critical Examination of Radioactive Dating of Rocks,"* Creation Research Society Quarterly Vol. 7, No. 3 137-141.

66. Koltz, J. W., *Genes, Genesis and Evolution* (St. Louis: Concordia Publishing, 1955) 208.

67. Simpson, G., *The History of Life in Evolution After Darwin.* (Chicago: University of Chicago Press, 1960) 143-144.

68. Leakey, R. E. F., *"Further Evidence of Lower Pleistocene Hominid from East Rudolf, North Kenya,"* Nature, Vol. 231:241.

69. Leakey, R. E. F., *National Geographic* Vol. 143:819.

70. Gish, Dr. Dwane, Professor of Natural Science, and Donald Patton, Geologist, and Dr. Carl Baugh, Paleoanthropology, *CBS Television Special Interview* 1992.

71. *"Update Article on Dragon Legends,"* Omega 1981:32.

72. Levinton, Jeffrey S., *"The Big Bang of Animal Evolution,"* Scientific American (Nov. 1992) 84-91.

73. Morris, H. M., *The Twilight of Evolution* (Grand Rapids: Baker Book House, 1963).

74. Monastery, Richard, *"Mysteries of the Orient,"* Discovery (April 1993) 38-48.

75. Nelson, Byron C., *Deluge Story in Stone* 167.

76. CBS Special, February 1993.

77. Custance, Arthur C., *Flood Traditions of the World,* 29-31 (1976).

78. Francis, Nelson W., *The Structure of American English* (1958).

79. *"Comparison of Oxygen Isotope Records from the Greenland Ice Cores,"* Nature, Vol. 364 & 366 (1993).

80. Hapgood, Charles H., *Earth's Shifting Crust* (New York: Pantheon Books, 1958) and *Maps of the Ancient Sea* (New York: Chilton Books, 1966).

81. White, John, *Polar Shift* (Virginia Beach: A. R. E. Press, 1994).

82. Thompkins, Peter, *Mysteries of the Mexican Pyramids* (London: Thames and Hudson, 1987).

83. *Holy Bible* references are from the King James translation, with transla- tions from *Strong's Exhaustive Concordance* by James H. Strong.

84. McDowell, Josh, *Evidence that Demands a Verdict,* Campus Crusade for Christ (1972).

85. Cremo, Michael A., and Richard L. Thompson, *Forbidden Archaeology* (Los Angeles: Bhaktivedanta Booktrust: 1996).

86. Sevemy, A. B., V. A. Kotov, and T. T. Tsap, *"Observations of Solar Pulsations,"* Nature Vol. 259 (1976).

87. Brooks, J. R., G. R. Isaak, and H. B. van der Raay, *"Observations of Free Oscillations of the Sun,"* Nature, Vol. 259 (1976).

88. National Research Council, *The decade of Discovery in Astronomy and Astrophysics.* (Washington, D. C.: National Academy Press, 1991).

89. Kartturen, H., P. Kroger, H. Oja, M. Poutanen, and K. J. Donner, *Fundamental Astronomy,* (Berlin, Germany: Springer-Verlag, 1987).

90. Strobel, Lee, *The Case for Christ,* Zondervan Publishing House, Grand Rapids Michigan, 1998.

91. Francisco, Clyde T., *Introducing the Old Testament,* Nashville Tennessee, Broadman Press, 1977.

92. Mathews, Kenneth A., *The New American Commentary— Genesis 1-11:26,* Broadman and Holman Publishers, 1996.

93. Ryrie, Charles C., *Basic Theology,* Chicago, Moody Press, 1999.

94. Criswell, W. A., *Book of Daniel,* Zondervan Publishing, Grand Rapids Mi, 1969.

95. Harrelson, Walter, *Interpreting the Old Testament,* Vanderbilt Univ, 1964.

96. Plaut, W. G., *The Torah,* Union of American Hebrew Congregations, N.Y., 1981.

97. Schroeder, Dr. Gerald, *The Science of God,* Free Press of Simon and Schuster, 1997.

98. Humphreys, Dr. D. Russell, *Starlight and Time,* Master Books, Green Forest Ar. 1997.

99. Erickson, Millard J., *Christian Doctrine,* Baker Book House, Grand Rapids Mich., 2000.

100. Kennedy, D. James Phd. *The Real Meaning of the Zodiac,* Coral Ridge, Ft. Lauderdale Florida, 1989

101. Chittick, Donald, E., Phd., *The Puzzle of Ancient Man,* Compass, Oregon, 2006.

102. Burney, Gerry, *Eden to Evil*—Target Truth Ministries. com., 2018.

103. Albright, William, *From the Stone Age to Christianity,* Doubleday – Anchor Books, Garden City, New York, 1953.

104. James, E.O., *The Ancient Gods,* Castle Books, Edison, N.J., 2004

105. Tetlow, Jim, and Oakland, Roger, and Meyers, Brad, *QUEEN OF ALL,* Eternal Publications, Fairport N.Y., 2006.

106. Hisslopt, Michael, *THE TWO BABYLONS*.

107. Missler, Chuck, *THE SWORD OF ALLAH*, Koinonia House, 1994.

108. Morey, Dr. Robert, *IS ALLAH OF THE QURAN THE TRUE UNIVERSAL GOD?*, faithdefenders.com, Orange Calif.

109. Moshay, G.J.O., *WHO IS THIS ALLAH?*, Dorchester House, Buks, U.K., 1994.

110. Jeffey, Arthur, *ISLAM, MUHAMMAD, AND HIS RELIGION*, Liberal Arts Press, New York, 1958.

111. Guilaume, Alfred, *ISLAM*, Penguin, 1956.

112. VanEss, John, *MEET THE ARAB*, New York, 1943.

113. Hisslopt, Alexander, *The Two Babylons,* New York, Loizeaux Brothers, 1959.

114. Tighe, Professor of History William J., Muhlenberg College, Touchstone Magazine, *Calculating Christmas,* Dec. 2003.

115. Missler, Dr. Chuck, *The Christmas Story*, Koinonia House, Coeur d'Alene, Idaho.

116. Maranatha Church, *Birth of Christ Recalculated*, versebyberse. org, 1998.

117. Freas, Chuck, *Birth of Jesus*, freas.ws/Chuck's Teachings, over 20 other references listed.

118. Lea, Thomas, *The New Testament*, pg. 91.

119. Huges, David, Astronomer Sheffield University, England.

120. Gordenberg, Gershom, *The End of Days*, Freepress, New York, 2000.

121. Grant, George, *The Blood of the Moon*, Wolgemoth and Hyatt, Brentwood Tenn., 1991.

122. Missler, Chuck, *The Sword of Allah*, Koinonia House, 1994.

123. Morey, Dr. Robert, *Is Allah of the Quran the True Universal God?*, Orange Calif., faithdefenders.com

124. Moshay, G.J.O., *Who is this Allah?*, Dorchester House, Buks, UK, 1994.

125. Warraq, Ibn, *Why Am I Not a Muslim?*, Prometheus, Amherst, 1995.

126. Jeffery, Arthur, *Islam, Muhammad and His Religion*, Liberal Arts Press, New York, 1958.

127. Houstsma, Arnold, Basset, *Encyclopedia of Islam*, Hartman, Lewis, Menage, Pellat, Schacht, Leiden, E.J. Brill, 1913.

128. Guilaume, Alfred, *Islam*, Penguin, 1956.

129. VanEss, John, *Meet the Arab*, New York, 1943.

130. Lasor, Isbe, *Biblical Illustrator*, Winter 2004-05, 591, pg 55.

131. Strobel, Lee, *The Case for the Real Jesus*, Zondervan, Grand Rapids, Mich, 2007, pgs. 157-188.

132. Woodrow, Ralph Edward, *Babylon Mystery Religion*, Evangelistic Assn., Box 124, Riverside Cal, 1992.

133. Bailey, Cyril, *The Legacy of Rome*, Oxford, Clarendon Press, 1923.

134. Layard, Austen Henry, *Nineveh and its Remains*, Ney York, Putnam, 1849.

135. Layard, Austen Henry, *Nineveh and Babylon*, New York, Harper and Brothers, 1853.

136. *The Catholic Encyclopedia*, New York, Robert Appleton Co., 1911.

137. Hunt, Dave, *Judgment Day: Islam*.

138. *Israel and the Nations*, The Berean Call, Bend Ore., 2006.

139. Zwemer, Samuel, M., *The Moslem Doctrine of God*, New York, 1905.

140. Lindsey, Hal, *The Everlasting Hatred*, Oradi House, 2002.

141. Burney, Gerry, *Eden to Evil,* Target Truth Ministries.com., 2018

142. Burney, Gerry, *Revelation, Apostasy, End-Times, & "This Generation"*, Xulon, 2013.

143. Burney, Gerry, *God's Plan /Satan's Plan*, Xulon, 2013.

144. Burney, Gerry, *The Book of Chronologies & Time Charts*, Target Truth Ministries.com, 2019

145. Horn, Thomas r., Johns PhD., Donald C., *The Gods Who Walk Among Us*, Huntington House, 1999

INDEX

CPSIA information can be obtained
at www.ICGtesting.com
Printed in the USA
FSHW012056051219